DATA SCIENCE WITH PYTHON

I0491798

Complete Guide To
Understanding Data
Analytics And Data Science
With Python Programming

Craig Berg

Introduction

Thank you for choosing to read this book on Data Science with Python.

In it, we are going to learn important data science elements such as:

❖ What is data science (and its importance)

❖ The different types of data scientists

❖ The tools every data scientist should have and learn how to use

❖ How to start using python for data science, and tons of other important elements

After reading this guide, you should have hands-on knowledge of how to use Python for data science purposes:

PS: I'd like your feedback. If you are happy with this book, please leave a review on Amazon.

Please leave a review for this book on Amazon by visiting the page below:

https://amzn.to/2VMR5qr

Your Gift

Let me help you master this and other programming stuff quickly.

Visit

https://bit.ly/codetutorials

To Find Out More

Table of Content

Section 1: A Basic Introduction To Data Science

Data science is the study of large amounts of data. It involves use of scientific methods, algorithms, patterns, and processes for data analysis with the intent being to discover patterns within the data. Data science mainly consists of mathematical statistics and scientific computations. It helps in the extraction of information from data sources such as structured and unstructured data.

In this book, we are going to learn how to perform data science using the python programming language, a programming language that every data scientist should master.

Data science comprises of the following aspects:

❖ Collecting the data

❖ Cleaning and analyzing the raw data

❖ Modeling the data using complex computational algorithms

❖ Visualizing the structured data

❖ Understanding and interpreting the data

❖ Making decisions from the information of the data

Why We Need Data Science

Several years ago, when organizations and businesses collected data, they would store it in simple books and spreadsheet programs. Nowadays, the data has become more complex, and interpreting the data to make business decisions has become more complex and more important, which is why organizations are now opting to use computers and complex algorithms to make sense of the data they collect.

The following are some of the important reasons why data science is important in our daily lives:

❖ Data science has helped ensure that we use raw data to make informed business decisions and predictions

❖ Data science has helped prevent certain crimes such as money fraud

❖ It helps with making faster and correct decisions

❖ We use it to create recommender systems for certain products

❖ It helps improve technologies such as self-driving cars

❖ We use data science to create intelligent machines used in medical, transportation, agriculture, and other fields

❖ It helps prevent substantial financial losses

Data science applies in many areas of life including areas such as social media and other important areas that relate to daily life.

Types Of Data Scientists

According to the latest surveys, data science has become the highest rated job. On sites such as Glassdoor, data scientists earn over $170,000 per annum. Data scientists are people who can use various statistical methods and machine learning algorithms to analyze and interpret data.

They are various types of data scientists based on what they do. They include:

❖ **Data Analyst:** A data analyst performs operations on huge amounts of data from mining, analyzing, and finding patterns and relationships between the data and then using this analysis to solve problems. Data analysts' core skills include MATLAB, Python, R, SQL, Data Mining, Mathematics etc.

❖ **Data Engineer:** Data engineers are responsible for maintaining the data architecture for the data projects.

❖ **Data Administrator:** Data administrators are responsible for managing databases for data analysis projects and ensuring security.

❖ **Machine Learning Professional:** These data professionals work with various machine learning algorithms such as regression, clustering, random forests, etc.

❖ **Business Analyst:** A business analyst acts as an intermediary between the executives and the IT department in a company.

Requirements For Data Science

To be a good data scientist, you need to meet a few key requirements. We can classify these requirements as technical and non-technical.

Technical Requirements

The technical requirements for data analysis are:

❖ **Mathematical Modelling:** This is important because data scientists use it to make vast and quick calculations and detect patterns within vast amounts of data.

❖ **Statistics:** Understanding of statistical methods such as deviations, mean, medians, etc. is helps a data scientist understand and interpret data.

❖ **Machine Learning:** Mastering the concept of machine learning and corresponding algorithms helps improve problem-solving techniques.

❖ **Computer Programming:** For one to become a competent data scientist, mastering at least one programming language is important. The most recommended programming languages for data science are R, Python, or Spark.

❖ **Database:** Deep understanding of databases such as SQL is essential for data science.

Non-Technical Requirements

The non-technical requirements for data analysis are

❖ **Critical thinking:** Finding various ways to solve a problem for efficiency is an essential skill for data science.

❖ **Curiosity:** The ability to question every aspect and result in data science is also an important skill that helps discover problems that are not easy to identify.

❖ **Communication skills:** Communication skills help data scientist because data science is a consultative field that involves communicating and working with others.

Tools For Data Science

The following are some of the tools required for data science operations.

❖ **Data Analysis:** Here, Programming languages such as Python, R, MATLAB, SAS, Jupyter Lab, R studio etc. come in very handy and are necessary—you need to master at least one programming language.

❖ **Data Storage:** You need to learn how to work with data storage tools such as SQL, Amazon Redshift, Informatica, Apache Hadoop, etc.

❖ **Data Visualization:** You need to learn how to work with data visualization tools such as Jupyter Lab, Cognos, Tableau, etc.

❖ **Machine learning tools:** Learning how to work with machine learning tools such as Apache Spark, Microsoft Azure ML studio, Apache Mahout, etc. will prove invaluable.Data science also has a lifecycle:

Data Science Lifecycle

The process of data science happens in various stages that together help achieve the most efficient result and conclusions. The following is the lifecycle of data science from the first to the last.

❖ **Discovery:** This is usually the first step in the data science process. It involves collecting and acquiring the required data from the appropriate sources using the correct methods. Data can be from various sources such as webserver logs, social media data mines, census etc.

❖ **Data Preparation:** The second stage is data preparation; it involves cleaning of the collected data, data reduction, data integration, and data transformation. This process is important as it provides cleaner data with minimal errors thus better predictions and accurate models.

❖ **Model Planning:** At this stage, the most appropriate method and technique is determined for finding the relations between input data. At this step, we use statistical formulas, SQL analysis formulas, SAS, etc. to determine the relations between data variables.

❖ **Model Building:** In this stage, we start the process of building the data model. It involves splitting the data into testing data and training data. This model development stage uses different techniques such as classification, clustering, regression, and associations. The training data created then become an invaluable part of developing the model and testing it against the training data once complete.

❖ **Operationalization:** This stage leads to the final model after training and testing; this stage additionally involves submitting the derived reports, code, briefings, and technical documents. After exhaustive testing, the model then goes into real production.

❖ **Communicate Results:** Once the model achieves the set goal, the findings and results then move on to the business team that goes about using the data model to make decisions.

Data science and business intelligence has a definite relationship:

Data Science Vs. Business Intelligence

The following are the various differences between data science and business intelligence:

❖ **Perception:** Business Intelligence involves looking backward while data science involves looking forward within the provided data.

❖ **Data Sources:** Business intelligence uses structured data for their operations, mainly SQL data, while data science relies on both structured and unstructured data such as logs, texts, and mined data.

❖ **Tools:** Business intelligence involves tools such as Microsoft BI, Pentaho while data science relies on tools such as Google TensorFlow, Python, and R.

❖ **Problem Solving Technique**: Business Intelligence uses Data Visualization and Statistics while data science involves Machine Learning, statistics, Graphs, Visualization.

Components Of Data Science

Data science has the following key components:

* **Statistics:** This is one of the most important components of data science. It involves collecting and organizing data.

* **Data Visualization:** This component involves graphical representation of the data collected for interpretation. It helps ease access of huge amounts of data in visual representations.

* **Machine Learning:** Machine learning is the backbone of data science. It involves the study of various algorithms that help make predictions about future occurrences from the collected data.

* **Advanced Computing:** Advanced computing is a key data science component. It involves the designing, debugging, and maintenance of a computer program's source code.

Application Of Data Science Applies To The Following Fields:

❖ **Gaming:** Machine-learning algorithms play a very important role in gaming. Top gaming companies such as Electronic Arts and Sony are increasingly using data science in their game development.

❖ **Transport:** Self-driving cars utilize a lot of machine learning algorithms and data science concepts.

❖ **Fraud Detection systems:** Systems such as bank fraud systems utilizes data science.

❖ **Healthcare:** Data science has significantly improved healthcare systems such as medical imaging analysis and virtual robotic doctors.

❖ **Internet:** Various aspects of the internet rely on data science. Various search engines such as Google, Yahoo, and Bing utilizes data science.

❖ **Recommender Systems:** Personalized recommendations offered on platforms such as YouTube, Netflix, and Amazon are courtesy of data science

❖ **Recognition Systems:** Image and Speech recognition systems rely on data science.

Now that you have a firmer idea of what data science is and how its use applies to daily life, let us move on to discussing how Python —the programming language— fits into data science.

Section 2: Python For Data Science

As we have learned so far, as an intended data scientist, one of the tools you must learn how to use is a computer programming language. In this book, we are going to learn how to use Python, one of the best programming languages for data science.

NOTE: To understand the basic data science concepts discussed in this guide, you need a basics understanding of python. This guide has a brief, python programming refresher section. With that mentioned, go out of your way to learn more about python programming from other resources.

Why Python For Data Science

Generally, there are many programming languages with most of them suited for use in data science —for a professional at least.

Given this, why should you use python for data science instead of other programming languages? Here are the various reasons why Python is such a great programming language especially for data science:

❖ **It is simple:** Python is one of the simplest computer programming languages in existence. It does not involve complex syntax or a lot of code; this makes it ideal for data science because it (data science) requires a lot of computation and code.

❖ **Vast Libraries:** Languages such as Ruby or R are very good for operations such as data cleaning and sorting. However, they do not have the libraries that python provides for data science and machine learning.

❖ **Cross-platform:** Python is cross platform. This means that if you develop a model on a Linux machine, you will not have to re-create it once you switch the development environment.

❖ **Data source:** Python provides a simple and ideal environment for working with external data sources such as logs, text, SQL, and spreadsheets. It also provides a good visual layout for data visualization.

❖ **Powerful:** Python is the Swiss army knife of computer programming languages. It has powerful functions that help in machine learning algorithms and data analytics.

❖ **Open-source:** Python is open source and thus its development is constant. It has great developer community support and thus regular updates.

Those are some of the advantages of python over other programming languages for data science.

To work with Python for data science, you need to install Python. The next section looks at this:

Section 3: Python Environment Setup

In this section, we are going to look at how to setup our python environment for data science.

NOTE: The working environment setup varies based on operating system and although this guide covers setup for most major Operating Systems, knowledge of working with the chosen operating system is essential.

Windows Environment Setup

In this section, we are going to setup our python environment for data science on the Microsoft Windows Operating system. For this setup, your computer should have the following minimum system requirements for ideal workspace:

❖ 4GB of RAM

❖ At least 5GB of free space

❖ An Internet connection and an active web browser

To setup the python environment, we are going to use the Python Anaconda distribution.

Anaconda is open source python and R distribution for scientific computing. It contains packages and libraries normally used in data science. It also has its own package management known as Conda used for installing and updating the python packages.

To install Anaconda, open the browser and navigate to the following page:

https://www.anaconda.com/distribution

Select the Windows installer for Python 3 and download the graphical installer. Once the download is complete, open the installer and follow the installation prompts.

NOTE: If you do not have another installation of the python programming language, select the option "Add anaconda to path" during the installation. Do not select this option if you have another python installation.

Once you have Anaconda installed, it will come with a development environment called Jupyter; this allows you to write code, display images, import data, and write notes. Jupyter is the most famous development environment for data science for both professionals and students

NOTE: You can use any python development environment —apart from Jupyter. However, this guide does not cover setup for other development environments.

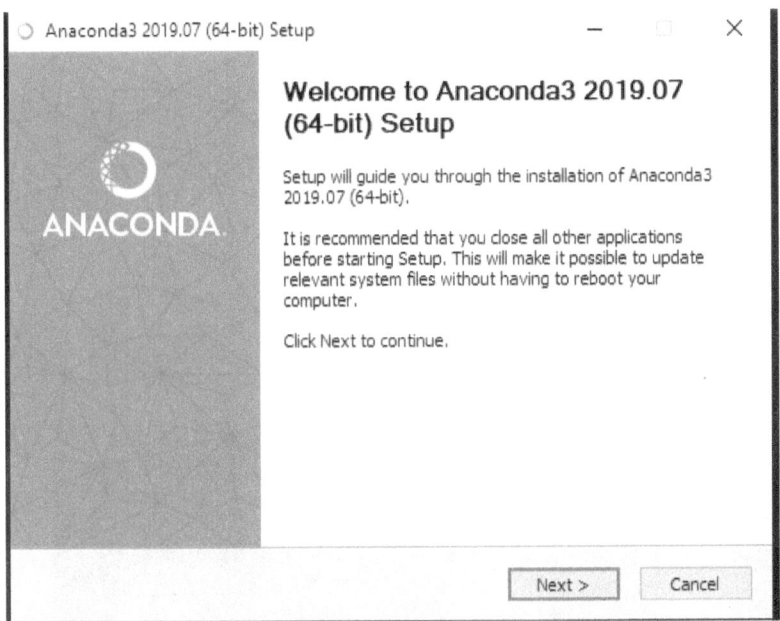

Linux Installation

By default, Linux distributions come with python pre-installed. However, the package installed by default is not ideal for data science and you need to install every library one at a time.

In addition, the version installed can be outdated and may thus trigger compatibility issues with the code used in this book. Navigate to anaconda download's page and download the installation package for Linux.

NOTE: For compatibility, ensure you download the latest version of Python 3.

Once the download is complete, open the Linux terminal and navigate to the directory of the download. Now enter the following commands in the terminal.

```
sudo    chmod    u+x    Anaconda3-2019.07-Linux-
x86_64.sh
```

```
art3mis37@Captain-PC:~$ cd Downloads/
art3mis37@Captain-PC:~/Downloads$ ls -l
total 529216
-rwxrw-rw- 1 art3mis37 art3mis37 541906131 Sep 23 14:37 Anaconda3-2019.07-Linux-x86_64.sh
art3mis37@Captain-PC:~/Downloads$ chmod u+x Anaconda3-2019.07-Linux-x86_64.sh
art3mis37@Captain-PC:~/Downloads$ bash ./Anaconda3-2019.07-Linux-x86_64.sh

Welcome to Anaconda3 2019.07

In order to continue the installation process, please review the license
agreement.
Please, press ENTER to continue
>>>
```

Next, execute the command below to start the anaconda installation. Ensure you have enough storage otherwise, the installation will not complete.

```
./Anaconda3-2019-07-Linux-x86_64.sh
```

Once the installation has initiated, accept the License agreement by entering yes in the terminal

```
Do you accept the license terms? [yes|no]
[no] >>> yes

Anaconda3 will now be installed into this location:
/home/art3mis37/anaconda3

  - Press ENTER to confirm the location
  - Press CTRL-C to abort the installation
  - Or specify a different location below

[/home/art3mis37/anaconda3] >>>
```

Follow the instructions provided by the installer and set them accordingly. Once the installation has completed, you can launch the Anaconda environment by executing anaconda-navigator command in the terminal.

Mac Environment Setup

For Apple users, the installation is very similar to the Windows installation if you are using the graphical installer. Download the package from Anaconda downloads page and launch it.

Follow the instructions —the default options are appropriate— and launch Anaconda once the installation has completed. If you choose to use the command-line installer instead, the operation is similar to that of Linux.

Now that our environment is ready, we need to look at its most important aspects. Head over to the next section for this:

Section 4: Environment Overview

In this section, we are going to look at the most important features of the python environment we setup in the last section. It is very important that we understand the workspace so that you can effectively troubleshoot any problems that arise.

To launch Anaconda, launch the Anaconda navigator from start menu or terminal for Mac or Linux users. Once you launch it, it will prompt the following window.

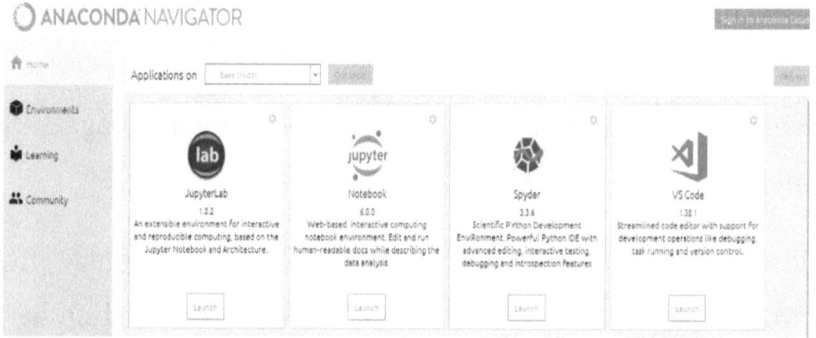

The most important tool we are going to focus on is the Jupyter Notebook. To launch the Jupyter notebook, you can use the Anaconda navigator or the Command prompt.

To launch it using the command prompt, enter the command `jupyter notebook`. Jupyter notebook will launch on your current directory in the command prompt.

For example, if the command prompt is in C:/users/Username, it will use that as the home directory. Once the command executes, it will launch a new browser window.

Now create a folder called Data-Science where we will put all the programming code used in this book. To create a new jupyter notebook, open the folder we created and under new, select Python 3. Once a new window opens, enter the name of the file under the untitled section and click 'save.'

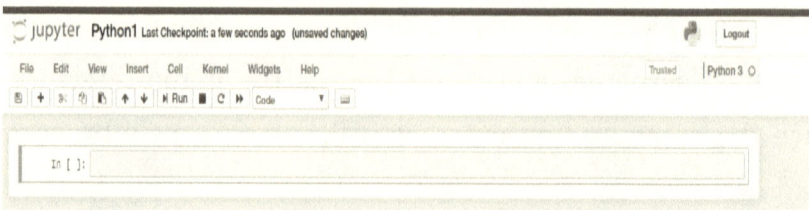

The box that opens is what we call a code cell. It allows one to enter python code and then run it. For example: enter the code `print("Hello world")`

Once you enter the code, you can run it by clicking SHIFT + RETURN. An output of the code will display and it shall create a new code cell as shown below.

To create a new cell below the run cell, you can use the ALT + RETURN key to create it. To save the notebook after working on it, you can use the CTRL + S or click the little floppy disk icon to save it. Jupyter notebook also has an auto save feature after two minutes or so.

If you want to download the code from the notebook in various formats such as .py, .html and .txt, you can click on file, download as, and select the format you wish to download as. Some formats may require installation of various packages.

On the other hand, if you encounter a code that is running forever, perhaps a code error or so, the cell with the code running will have an asterisk. To interrupt the execution, look at the top bar, select Kernel, and select Restart kernel. To get more information on Jupyter notebook in general and other libraries from the Anaconda distribution, you can use the help option in the top menu.

Anaconda Virtual Environments

This advanced subsection covers how to create anaconda virtual environments. Anaconda virtual environments allow the setup and configuration of python and various libraries.

For example, if you have a default Anaconda python 3 installation, you can create a virtual environment that runs python 2 without affecting the other installations. You can also install libraries to the virtual environment, activate, deactivate, and delete it whenever necessary.

Instances of where you may need to create a virtual environment include:

1. When you create a python program that runs on a certain version of a library

2. A new version of the library you used is released

3. You want to test out the code using the latest release and do not want the previous code to break. You can create virtual environment with the latest release and test it out without affecting the older code.

To find out more about virtual environments using the anaconda distribution, navigate to the following resource page:

https://bit.ly/2nKw5le

Launch the command prompt to start creating virtual environments. Do not open the command prompt as admin as it will create the virtual environments in the %systemroot%system32 directory.

Once you launch the command prompt, enter the following command

```
conda create - -name TestEnv Pandas
```

The above code creates a virtual environment called TestEnv and associates the Pandas library with it. Anaconda gets the package metadata and all the required libraries to install.

```
C:\Users\capta>conda create --name TestEnv pandas
Collecting package metadata (current_repodata.json): done
Solving environment: done


==> WARNING: A newer version of conda exists. <==
  current version: 4.7.10
  latest version: 4.7.12

Please update conda by running

    $ conda update -n base -c defaults conda
```

Once you accept the packages you want installed, it shall install the packages and create the virtual environment.

```
The following NEW packages will be INSTALLED:

  blas              pkgs/main/win-64::blas-1.0-mkl
  ca-certificates   pkgs/main/win-64::ca-certificates-2019.8.28-0
  certifi           pkgs/main/win-64::certifi-2019.9.11-py37_0
  icc_rt            pkgs/main/win-64::icc_rt-2019.0.0-h0cc432a_1
  intel-openmp      pkgs/main/win-64::intel-openmp-2019.4-245
  mkl               pkgs/main/win-64::mkl-2019.4-245
  mkl-service       pkgs/main/win-64::mkl-service-2.3.0-py37hb782905_0
  mkl_fft           pkgs/main/win-64::mkl_fft-1.0.14-py37h14836fe_0
  mkl_random        pkgs/main/win-64::mkl_random-1.0.2-py37h343c172_0
  numpy             pkgs/main/win-64::numpy-1.16.5-py37h19fb1c0_0
  numpy-base        pkgs/main/win-64::numpy-base-1.16.5-py37hc3f5095_0
  openssl           pkgs/main/win-64::openssl-1.1.1d-he774522_0
  pandas            pkgs/main/win-64::pandas-0.25.1-py37ha925a31_0
  pip               pkgs/main/win-64::pip-19.2.2-py37_0
  python            pkgs/main/win-64::python-3.7.4-h5263a28_0
  python-dateutil   pkgs/main/win-64::python-dateutil-2.8.0-py37_0
  pytz              pkgs/main/noarch::pytz-2019.2-py_0
  setuptools        pkgs/main/win-64::setuptools-41.2.0-py37_0
  six               pkgs/main/win-64::six-1.12.0-py37_0
  sqlite            pkgs/main/win-64::sqlite-3.29.0-he774522_0
  vc                pkgs/main/win-64::vc-14.1-h0510ff6_4
  vs2015_runtime    pkgs/main/win-64::vs2015_runtime-14.16.27012-hf0eaf9b_0
  wheel             pkgs/main/win-64::wheel-0.33.6-py37_0
  wincertstore      pkgs/main/win-64::wincertstore-0.2-py37_0

Proceed ([y]/n)? y
```

To activate the created environment, we use the command `conda activate TestEnv`

You can also deactivate using the command `conda deactivate TestEnv`

```
C:\Users\capta>conda activate TestEnv
(TestEnv) C:\Users\capta>
```

To test the difference between this environment and the base Python environment, try importing modules that do not exist. For example, the TestEnv environment created was using the Pandas package. If we try to import a package that does not exist such as matplotlib, it will result in an error as shown.

```
(TestEnv) C:\Users\capta>python
Python 3.7.4 (default, Aug  9 2019, 18:34:13) [MSC v.1915 64 bit (AMD64)] :: Anaconda, Inc. on win32
Type "help", "copyright", "credits" or "license" for more information.
>>> import pandas as pd
>>> from matplotlib import pyplot as plt
Traceback (most recent call last):
  File "<stdin>", line 1, in <module>
ModuleNotFoundError: No module named 'matplotlib'
>>>
```

This is because the virtual environment TestEnv does not have the matplotlib library installed. To install it on the virtual environment, you can use the `conda install matplotlib` command.

To create an environment with a different version of python, you can use the command `conda create -name Python2Version python=2.7 <library-name>`

This creates a virtual environment that is running python 2 with a library as you specified above. Virtual environments have more applications and uses.

To use Python for data science, you need to understand a few python programming elements. The next section of the guide gives you a refresher of the most important python programming elements you need to know before we can start using Python to work with data:

Section 5: Python Refresher Section

In this section, we are going to get an overview of the most important python concepts used in this guidebook.

The following are some of the topics we are going to cover in this section.

- ❖ Data types

- ❖ Control Flow

- ❖ Operators

- ❖ Loops

- ❖ List Comprehensions

- ❖ Functions

- ❖ Lambda Expressions

- ❖ Maps and Filters

Section 5a: Data Types

In this first subsection, we are going to discuss the basic data types supported by the python programming language.

Go ahead and launch the Jupyter notebook; once launched, open the folder DataScience we created previously. In that folder, create a new folder called pythonRefresher. Now create a notebook called section1 where we are going to enter all the code.

Let us get started with numbers and basic arithmetic.

Python supports two number types: integers and floating-point numbers. Integers are basic whole numbers without decimals such as 2, 3, or 4. Floating-point numbers are numbers with decimals such as 2.33, 23.01, or 4.00. Both number types support all arithmetic operations such as addition, subtraction, multiplication, etc.

NOTE: Differences may arise for Python 2 and Python 3 users while performing various operations such as division and exponents.

Like most programming languages, python follows a specific order while performing these operations with the higher precedence being the brackets, multiplication and division, then addition and subtraction.

Python uses the mod function – denoted as % - to get the remainder after a division operation. For example, 4 % 2 = 0. This means that 4 divided by 2 is 2 with no remainder. The mod function is a very good way to check for even numbers since an even number % 2 is never 0.

Now let us move on to variable assignment.

If you want to pick a variable name to assign a certain value, you must follow the rules of naming variables. The assignment operator in python is just a single equal sign. For example:

```
age = 20
```

The rules of naming a variable are as follows:

❖ Variable cannot contain a python keyword

❖ Variables cannot start with a number or a special character

❖ Variable names should not contain spaces or special characters except an underscore _

Other languages use periods to separate names. For python, use the underscore or stick to camel Casing.

Let us move on to strings.

In python, there are two main ways to create a string. The first method is using single quotes to enclose the part of the string and the second method is to use double quotes. Another method can be to wrap opposite quotes inside each other. For example, `"That is James' book"`

The correct way to print output in python is to use the print() function instead of calling the variable name. For example, if we have a variable called `myStrig` = `"Hello"`. If you call `myString`, it will print out 'Hello' with single quotes. However, if you call `print(myString)`, it will print hello without quotes.

There are several ways you can format your print statement. For example, if you have a variable called num = 10 and name = "John." If you want to print an output based off the variables above, we use string formatting in python.

```
"The value of the numbe is {} and the name is {} ". format (num, name)
```

This formatting technique is ideal when compared to the use of % sign. For example:

```
"The value of the number is %number and the name is %name"%num, name
```

Indexing strings is another concept supported by python strings. If you have a string called var = "Hello," the string var is just a sequence of characters. Each character represents an individual element in the string. You can fetch each element in the string using the square bracket notation. The indexing in python starts at index 0. For example, to get the character in position 3:

`var[2]` which returns the value l

Python also supports slice notation to get slices of a string. If we have a string that contains all the alphabetical letters, we can get all the letters from index 10 to beyond as shown below:

```
var = "ABCDEFGHIJKLMNOPQRSTUVWXYZ"
```

```
var[10::]
```
```
'KLMNOPQRSTUVWXYZ'
```

The reverse is also true meaning you can get the values index 0 to a certain index.

```
var[:5]
```
```
'ABCDE'
```

This tells python to grab everything from index 0 up to but not including index 5.

Let us go ahead and discuss lists, which use similar concepts as strings. To create a string in python, we use the square brackets as shown below:

```
my_list = [1,2,3,4,5,6,7]
```

```
print(my_list)
[1, 2, 3, 4, 5, 6, 7]
```

Python lists can support any data type such as numbers, strings, tuples, and even nested lists. Lists are not very different from strings as they are just a sequence of elements separated by commas. To add elements at the end of the list, you use the .append() function. For example:

```
my_list.append(90)
```

```
print(my_list)
[1, 2, 3, 4, 5, 6, 7, 90]
```

The slicing notation for lists is identical that of strings. To grab elements from a specific index, we use my_list[o:6]

Section 5b: Dictionaries And Tuples

In this section, we are going to discuss dictionaries and tuples. To create a dictionary in python, we use the curly brackets followed by the dictionary key and its corresponding value separated by a colon. For example:

```
my_dict = {"Key1":"value1", "key2": 100}
```

```
print(my_dict)
{'Key1': 'value1', 'key2': 100}
```

Dictionaries are identical to hash tables as they behave as key value pairs. Instead of holding the elements in sequence, they hold the elements in keys and then their corresponding values. This means that referencing dictionaries using indexes such as `my_dict[0]` will result in an error. To use a certain element in a dictionary, we use the dictionary key. For example: `my_dict["key2"]`

```
my_dict["key2"]
100
```

Python dictionaries can hold any data type including other dictionaries inside them as their values. For example:

```
dictionary = {'key1':{'insideKey':[4,5,6]}, "key2":{"innerKey": [5,6,7]}}
```

```
print(dictionary)
```

```
{'key1': {'insideKey': [4, 5, 6]}, 'key2': {'innerKey': [5, 6, 7]}}
```

Dictionaries do not contain any order as they just contain key value mappings.

Let us move on to booleans in python.

Python booleans are simple since they are just true and false. Their main use is to test for logical values; we normally chain them with other python operators.

Tuples in python are close to lists except they use parenthesis instead of square brackets.

```
my_tuple = (1,2,3,4)
```

```
type(my_tuple)
```

```
tuple
```

You can also perform operations such as indexing using the same technique in lists using square brackets notation. The key difference between tuples and lists is that tuples are immutable, which means you cannot reassign a value once you declare it.

```
my_list[0] = "First"
```

```
print(my_list)
```

```
['First', 2, 3, 4, 5, 6, 7, 90]
```

```
my_tuple[0] = "First"
```

```
---------------------------------------------------------------------
TypeError                              Traceback (most recent call last)
<ipython-input-18-5ed22c9fe338> in <module>
----> 1 my_tuple[0] = "First"

TypeError: 'tuple' object does not support item assignment
```

Python set is a collection of unique elements. We use curly braces similar to dictionaries except it does not have a key and a value. For example:

```
my_set = {1,2,3,4,5}
```

```
type(my_set)
```

```
set
```

If you add similar numbers within a set, it removes all the duplicates and only uses the unique value. For example:

```
my_set = {1,2,3,2,4,2,1,4,3,6,5,7,5,6,7,4,3,3,2,5,7}
```

```
print(my_set)
```

```
{1, 2, 3, 4, 5, 6, 7}
```

This is because sets are defined by unique elements within it. If you have a list containing duplicates, you can use the set function to return the unique values within it. You can also add elements to a set by using the .add() function provided the element you want to add is not a duplicate of another value within the set.

Let us move on to operators in python.

We use comparison operators in python —and most other programming languages— to compare values and results of expressions against the other.

They include:

❖ Greater than

❖ Less

❖ Less than or equal to

❖ Greater than or equal to

❖ Equal to

❖ Not equal to

The result of comparison operators is a Boolean. For example:

```
10 > 20
```

```
False
```

The above test results into a Boolean False

You can also use comparison operators in conjuction with strings and not just numbers. However, the string comparison must match even in upper and lower casings.

On the other hand, Logic operators combine the comparison operators to result in a single Boolean result. The code below is an example of a logical operator.

```
a = 2
```

```
b  = 10
```

```
a >b and b < a
```

Logical operators include:

* ❖ Logical AND

* ❖ Logical OR

* ❖ Logical NOT

For the expression to result in true using the logical and, all the expressions must evaluate to true; otherwise, the result is false. For the case of logical OR, one of the expression must be true for the expression to be true otherwise the result becomes false.

The not operator returns the negative of the overall result. If the result evaluates to true, the not operators returns a false and vice versa.

The next part is python conditionals.

To execute a certain code if a certain condition evaluates to true, we use the if, elif, and else statements. For example:

```
score = 60
if (score >= 70):
    print("Excellent")
elif(score >= 60):
    print("Good")
else:
    print("Try Harder")
```

Good

The score is set to 60 and the code below it tells python that if the score is greater than or equal to 70, perform this action. Otherwise, if the score is greater than or equal to 60, perform this action; otherwise, execute this code. You can have as many nested if and elif statements as required. Remember to keep your code clean instead of nesting many conditionals.

Section 5c: Loops And Functions

In this section, we are going to cover python features such as loops and some of the python functions. Python supports two types of loops: for loops and while loops. For loops allow you to perform iteration through a sequence. For example, if you have a list with certain number of elements, you can use a for loop to perform operations in the list.

```
for items in my_list:
    print(items)
```
```
1
2
3
4
5
6
7
8
```

The temporary variable items can be whatever you want it to be. However, you cannot use it outside the loop, as it is only available inside the called loop. The action of a for loop does not have to be related to the elements within the specified list.

While loops continue performing a set of code if the condition is true; on the other hand, execution of while loops stops when after the specified condition evaluates to false.

```
x = 10
while x < 100:
    print("The value of x is {}".format(x))
    x = x +1
```

```
The value of x is 10
The value of x is 11
The value of x is 12
The value of x is 13
The value of x is 14
The value of x is 15
The value of x is 16
The value of x is 17
The value of x is 18
The value of x is 19
The value of x is 20
```

This prints all the values from 10 to 100. If you skip the x = x +1 code, the code will run forever as the condition will never turn to false. That section of the code increase x by 1 every time an iteration occurs.

Functions are a helpful python feature. Let us discuss some of the useful functions in python.

One useful function in python is the range() function. We use the range function to generate numerical values given the start and ending point. The most common use of the range function is in the for loop. For example, to print values from 10 to 50:

```
for i in range(10, 50):
    print(i)
    i = i+1
```

Another useful function is the list() function that allows you to convert certain elements into a python string. For example:

```
print(list(range(10,50)))
```

[10, 11, 12, 13, 14, 15, 16, 17, 18, 19, 20, 21, 22, 23, 24, 25, 26, 27, 28, 29, 30, 31, 32, 33, 34, 35, 36, 37, 38, 39, 40, 41, 42, 43, 44, 45, 46, 47, 48, 49]

This converts the generated values from the range function into a list. Other important python functions include:

❖ dict()

❖ round()

❖ min()

❖ max()

❖ abs()

❖ len()

❖ type()

We can also create our own functions in python. Functions allow us to reuse a block of code without having to rewrite the code. To use a function in python, we first declare the function and its corresponding code operation and then call the function whenever necessary. We do a function declaration using the def keyword followed by the function name, parameters in the parenthesis and then the code we want executed:

```
def my_function(parameter1):
    print(parameter1)
```

```
my_function("Hello")
```

```
Hello
```

The above function is a very simple concept of how functions should work.

In terms of parameters, a python function can have more than o parameters. This means that functions do not necessarily have to contain parameters. Remember that when calling a function, we add parenthesis at the end of the function name. If you do not, this will just return the type of the object, which in this case is a function with one parameter

There are other cases where you want a function to return a value after its operation. For example, if you create a function that calculates the maximum value between two numbers, you will want to return the maximum value as shown below:

```python
def max_value(num1, num2):
    if num1 > num2:
        maximum = num1
    else:
        maximum = num2
    return maximum
```

```python
max_value(10,20)
```

```
20
```

You can then use the returned value from the function to perform a certain operation or assign it to another variable.

If you want to add a documentation in a python string, you can add three colons at the start and end of the documentation. For example, to tell someone what the max_value function does, you just do:

```
def max_value(num1, num2):
    """This function takes two number as arguments and returns the maxim valeu"""
    if num1 > num2:
        maximum = num1
    else:
        maximum = num2
    return maximum
```

Section 5d: Expressions And Methods

In this section, we are going to discuss map and filter functions, and then lambda expressions followed by the methods we can use against certain data types in python.

In python, Map functions take two arguments: the function to use as well as the times to iterate through each iterable object, and the data type to use. For example, if we have a list with numerical elements such as my_list = [1,2,3,4,5,6,7]

We can call the map function by passing the function we want to use and the data as shown below:

```
def multiply_by_2(value):
    return value*2
```

```
my_list = [1,2,3,4,5,6,7]
```

```
map(multiply_by_2, my_list)
```

```
<map at 0x2318fe516d8>
```

Once we can the map function, python will tell us the location of the created map in the memory. If you want to cast the result of the map into a list, you can cast the map result into a list using the built-in list function. The result will be a list with each element of the previous list with the operation of the passed function. In this case, it returns a list with all the elements in the my_list multiplied by 2.

```
list(map(multiply_by_2, my_list))
```
```
[2, 4, 6, 8, 10, 12, 14]
```

Lambda expressions come in handy at this aspect.

In most cases, the map function will be a one-time thing and you do not necessarily have to define and create a new function just to use for the map operation. Lambda expressions allow us to write a function such as `multiply_by2_2` in one line and for use in that one case. We also call Lambda expressions anonymous expression because we normally use them without naming.

If we want to re-write the multiply_by_2 function, we get rid of certain features such as the def keyword, the name of the function, and the return keyword. In the final scenario, we end up with `lambda value:value*2`

```
lambda value:value*2
```

```
<function __main__.<lambda>(value)>
```

You can also allocate the value of a lambda expression to a variable for example:

```
Func_name = lambda value:value*2
```

Use of Lambda expressions is very common in the map function where instead of defining an entire function, we just use a lambda expression. For example:

```
list(map(lambda value:value*3, my_list))
```

```
[3, 6, 9, 12, 15, 18, 21]
```

The filter function in python is similar to a python map function in terms of the structure. However, it does not map every element to the specified sequence; instead, it filters elements from a given sequence.

For example, if we call the filter function, we pass in the function or create a lambda expression followed by the sequence of elements to use. The result of filter function is a series of boolean values. For example, we can filter the even values in a given sequence as follows:

```
list(filter(lambda value:value%2 == 0, my_list))
```

```
[2, 4, 6]
```

This returns all the even values within the specified sequence.

Now let us go ahead and discuss the various methods you can call based on the data type in python. For strings, the important methods include:

* .lower() method : This converts the string to lower case

* .upper() : This converts the string to upper case

* .split() : This splits the string on all the corresponding whitespaces in the string

* .replace() : This replaces an older string with a new string

For dictionaries, important methods include:

* .keys() : This returns all the keys available in the specified dictionary

* .items() This returns all the items in the dictionary

* .clear() : This deletes everything from the called dictionary

For python lists, the following are the most useful python methods

❖ .pop : This removes the last item in a list. Changes made by this method are permanent

❖ .apped() : This adds a new item in the list

There are other supported methodss for lists and other python data types. If you are a beginner in programming in general, aim to learn as much as you can about python programming.

Now you have a firmer idea of the most important bits about python programming necessary for data science. Let us move on:

Section 6: Working With Python For Data Analysis

In Python programming, data analysis is the method of collecting, cleaning, and analyzing data using scientific data analysis tools such as:

NumPy

NumPy is a Python Linear Library used in scientific computing, machine learning, and data analysis. It comprises of multidimensional array objects and routines for processing arrays. NumPy, which stands for Numerical Python, is very essential in data analysis.

NumPy provides the following operations

❖ Ndarrays – fast and space-efficient array objects that represent multidimensional and homogenous items. It also provides arithmetic operations and classy broadcasting capabilities.

❖ Linear algebraic expressions and Fourier number translations

❖ Integration of C and C++ code

* Tools for working with memory-shaped files

* Reads and writes arrays to and from disks.

* Provides fast and accurate mathematical functions without re-writing loops

NumPy itself does not provide high-level data analytics capabilities; nevertheless, it is very important that you have a firm understanding of NumPy arrays array computing as having this knowledge helps build up other library knowledge such as Pandas.

Data analysis mainly focuses on the following operations:

* Array operations for data cleaning, sub setting, filtering, and transformation

* Array algorithms such as sorting and set procedures

* Conditional logical array expressions

* Group data manipulation

* Relational data manipulation

* Data alignment

Installing NumPy

To get NumPy installed on the computer, use the Anaconda distribution as it comes prepackaged with this library. However, if you are using another installation of python or using miniconda, you can install it by running:

```
python -m pip install numpy
```

```
conda install numpy
```

For numpy, we are going to use NumPy arrays in the book. We are going to focus on the two flavors of the numpy arrays: vector and matrices numpy arrays also known as ndarrays.

NumPy Arrays

For this part, we are going to look at ways to create and work with NumPy arrays. Open the Jupyter notebook and create a notebook called NumPy under the DataScience folder we created earlier. We can create a NumPy array from the pre-existing python objects such as lists. The first step is to import NumPy as follows:

```
my_list = [100,200,300]
```

```
my_list
```

```
[100, 200, 300]
```

```
import numpy as np
```

```
my_array = np.array(my_list)
```

```
type(my_array)
```

```
numpy.ndarray
```

First, we create a list with three elements. We then imported numpy and called np. We can then call the .array() function off the list and assign it to a new variable. As you can see, the type of the array is of type numpy.ndarray, which is a single dimensional array vector

Casting a single list as an array returns a single dimensional array. To get a two dimensional matrix, you can cast a list within a list as follows:

```
matrix = [[100,200,300],[400,500,600],[700,800,900]]
```

```
matrix
```

```
[[100, 200, 300], [400, 500, 600], [700, 800, 900]]
```

```
np.array(matrix)
```

```
array([[100, 200, 300],
       [400, 500, 600],
       [700, 800, 900]])
```

This creates a multi-dimensional matrix of 3 rows and 3 columns shown by the output and by the number of brackets.

Numpy also provides its own built function for generating random values into ndarrays. The most common way is using the. arange() function. This function is like the python built-in range () function. The np.arange() function takes various arguments: a start, a stop, a step, and the type as shown below:

```
np.arange(0,11)
```

```
array([ 0,  1,  2,  3,  4,  5,  6,  7,  8,  9, 10])
```

This creates an array of values from 0 up to but not including 11. If you want all the even values from 0 to 11, you can add the step size as 2 as shown below:

```
In [12]:  np.arange(0,11,2)

Out[12]:  array([ 0,  2,  4,  6,  8, 10])
```

We can use other methods to generate special types of arrays. For example, if you want to generate an array of zeros, you can use the .zeros method as shown:

```
np.zeros((4,5))
array([[0., 0., 0., 0., 0.],
       [0., 0., 0., 0., 0.],
       [0., 0., 0., 0., 0.],
       [0., 0., 0., 0., 0.]])
```

You can pass a single value to generate a single dimensional vector of the values specified or pass a tuple to create a multi-dimensional matrix of the values specified. The first value in the passed tuple represents the number of rows and the second number represents the number of columns of the matrix.

You can also create an array of ones by using the .ones() function. For example:

```
np.ones(5)
```

```
array([1., 1., 1., 1., 1.])
```

```
np.ones((4,5))
```

```
array([[1., 1., 1., 1., 1.],
       [1., 1., 1., 1., 1.],
       [1., 1., 1., 1., 1.],
       [1., 1., 1., 1., 1.]])
```

Another useful function supported by the numpy arrays is linspace() which creates a series of evenly distributed numbers over a specified interval. Do not confuse linspace with arange.

```
np.linspace(0,10,100)
```

```
array([ 0.        ,  0.1010101 ,  0.2020202 ,  0.3030303 ,  0.4040404 ,
        0.50505051,  0.60606061,  0.70707071,  0.80808081,  0.90909091,
        1.01010101,  1.11111111,  1.21212121,  1.31313131,  1.41414141,
        1.51515152,  1.61616162,  1.71717172,  1.81818182,  1.91919192,
        2.02020202,  2.12121212,  2.22222222,  2.32323232,  2.42424242,
        2.52525253,  2.62626263,  2.72727273,  2.82828283,  2.92929293,
        3.03030303,  3.13131313,  3.23232323,  3.33333333,  3.43434343,
        3.53535354,  3.63636364,  3.73737374,  3.83838384,  3.93939394,
        4.04040404,  4.14141414,  4.24242424,  4.34343434,  4.44444444,
        4.54545455,  4.64646465,  4.74747475,  4.84848485,  4.94949495,
        5.05050505,  5.15151515,  5.25252525,  5.35353535,  5.45454545,
        5.55555556,  5.65656566,  5.75757576,  5.85858586,  5.95959596,
        6.06060606,  6.16161616,  6.26262626,  6.36363636,  6.46464646,
        6.56565657,  6.66666667,  6.76767677,  6.86868687,  6.96969697,
        7.07070707,  7.17171717,  7.27272727,  7.37373737,  7.47474747,
        7.57575758,  7.67676768,  7.77777778,  7.87878788,  7.97979798,
        8.08080808,  8.18181818,  8.28282828,  8.38383838,  8.48484848,
        8.58585859,  8.68686869,  8.78787879,  8.88888889,  8.98989899,
        9.09090909,  9.19191919,  9.29292929,  9.39393939,  9.49494949,
        9.5959596 ,  9.6969697 ,  9.7979798 ,  9.8989899 , 10.        ])
```

This creates an arrays of 100 random numbers between 0 and 10. This makes a quick way of creating test data for modeling. The array looks like a two dimensional array but it is actually a single dimensional indicated by the number of square brackets.

The difference between arange and linspace is the third argument. arange will take the third argument as the step size while linspace will take the third argument as the number or points the array will contain.

You can also create an identity matrix using numpy. An identity matrix, also called a square or unit matrix, is a type of matrix where the main diagonal consists of 1s and the rest are 0s. Identity matrix is a very useful matrix when dealing with linear algebra problems. To create an identity matrix using numpy, you can call the eye() followed by the number as the number of rows and columns. For example:

```
In [14]: np.eye(5)

Out[14]: array([[1., 0., 0., 0., 0.],
                [0., 1., 0., 0., 0.],
                [0., 0., 1., 0., 0.],
                [0., 0., 0., 1., 0.],
                [0., 0., 0., 0., 1.]])
```

Numpy also contains various ways to create an array of random numbers –we may use these function very often in the book.

The most common way is to use the random function. The random function contains numerous methods such as rand, randint, operator, np randn, etc. Let us go ahead and discuss the commonly used method for generating random numbers. `np.random.rand()` – it is used to create an array of a given shape passed as a paramter by populating it with random data from uniform distribution between 0 and 1.

```
np.random.rand(5)
```

```
array([0.92610988, 0.68075856, 0.73338999, 0.35995416, 0.17470212])
```

```
np.random.rand(5,5)
```

```
array([[0.8888736 , 0.13260588, 0.57677921, 0.11841044, 0.84895103],
       [0.55251345, 0.90035991, 0.14988986, 0.1508782 , 0.11892481],
       [0.46470614, 0.36829021, 0.08404968, 0.1242882 , 0.5622558 ],
       [0.27342778, 0.1515617 , 0.46492156, 0.138038  , 0.5975308 ],
       [0.8696446 , 0.02476652, 0.47905294, 0.96904722, 0.58799553]])
```

When creating multidimensional array using the rand method, we do not pass the columns and rows as tuples but just as single values as shown above.

If we want to create an array with sample data from normal standard distribution also known as gaussian distribution, we use the randn method instead of the rand method.

```
np.random.randn(6)
```
```
array([ 0.56925006, -0.40122954,  0.83953516, -1.11495608,  1.52010696,
        0.28892519])
```

You can also generate random integers based off a high and low value using the randint method. For example, to generate random numbers between 1 and 100, we use:

```
np.random.randint(0,100,10)

array([31, 75, 89, 32, 40, 88, 80, 75, 68, 11])
```

This generates 10 random numbers between 1 and 100.

Now let us go ahead and discuss attributes and methods of numpy arrays. Let us create an array object called my_array

```
my_array = np.arange(30)

my_arr = np.random.randint(0,50,10)

my_array
array([ 0,  1,  2,  3,  4,  5,  6,  7,  8,  9, 10, 11, 12, 13, 14, 15, 16,
       17, 18, 19, 20, 21, 22, 23, 24, 25, 26, 27, 28, 29])

my_arr
array([31, 38, 38, 44, 36, 24, 21, 40, 16, 11])
```

The first method we can use is the reshape() method. This method returns the arrays with the same data but different shape. For example, we can reshape the my_array – which contains 30 elements – into 6 rows and 5 columns as shown below:

```
my_array.reshape(5,6)
```

```
array([[ 0,  1,  2,  3,  4,  5],
       [ 6,  7,  8,  9, 10, 11],
       [12, 13, 14, 15, 16, 17],
       [18, 19, 20, 21, 22, 23],
       [24, 25, 26, 27, 28, 29]])
```

If it is not possible to divide the values in the array evenly to fill the matrix, python will result in an error:

```
my_array.reshape(6,6)
```

```
------------------------------------------------------------------
ValueError                        Traceback (most recent call last)
<ipython-input-27-6c7aa2ebf2d8> in <module>
----> 1 my_array.reshape(6,6)

ValueError: cannot reshape array of size 30 into shape (6,6)
```

To find the maximum value of a given array, we can use the .max() method off the array. For example, to get the maximum value of the random array my_arr, we call:

```
my_arr.max()
```

44

You can also find the minimum value by calling the min() method off the array.

To find out the index location of the max and min value, we call off the argmax and argmin off the array as shown:

```
my_arr.argmax()
```

3

```
my_arr.argmin()
```

9

We can also find out the shape of the vector by calling the .shape attribute.

```
my_arr.shape
```

(10,)

This means that the array is a one-dimensional vector containing 10 elements within it. You can also use the .dtype attribute to find the data type of the specified array – which in this case contains 32-bit integers.

```
my_array.dtype
```

```
dtype('int32')
```

NumPy Indexing and Selection

In this part, we are going cover how to select elements or groups of elements from a numpy array. Launch jupyter notebook and import numpy as np.

Let us start by creating an array using the arrange function that contains 15 elements from 0 up to 14

```
import numpy as np

my_array = np.arange(0,15)

my_array
array([ 0,  1,  2,  3,  4,  5,  6,  7,  8,  9, 10, 11, 12, 13, 14])
```

Elements in a numpy array are accessible through indexing and slicing just like any other python container object.

Numpy array indexing is zero-based and thus, the first element takes index 0. Indexing methods in python are field index, basic slice, and advanced index. We use square brackets and index notation to do this.

To get the value at index 10, we pass the array name and the index number in square brackets as shown below:

```
my_array[10]
```

```
10
```

To get elements in a range, we can specify the starting and the ending index to get the elements in that range. For example:

```
my_array[5:13]
```

```
array([ 5,  6,  7,  8,  9, 10, 11, 12])
```

In this case, it returns the values from index 5 to index 13. We can also skip the starting or the ending point to indicate that we want to grab everything before or after the specified array. For example, to get all values up to index 9, we call:

```
my_array[:9]
```

```
array([0, 1, 2, 3, 4, 5, 6, 7, 8])
```

```
my_array[6:]
```

```
array([ 6,  7,  8,  9, 10, 11, 12, 13, 14])
```

Let us look at an important part of numpy array called slicing. We can we create a variable that contains a slice of a certain array as shown:

```
slice_array = my_array[:6]
```

```
slice_array
```

```
array([0, 1, 2, 3, 4, 5])
```

The above array contains a slice of the main array with only 5 elements. We can broadcast a certain value to the slice array such as:

```
slice_array[:] = 100
```

```
slice_array
```

```
array([100, 100, 100, 100, 100, 100])
```

The slice of array now contains a series of 5, 100 values. If you try to call the main array that the slice_array is part of, it will contain the values broadcasted and not the original values:

```
my_array

array([100, 100, 100, 100, 100, 100,   6,   7,   8,   9,  10,  11,  12,
        13,  14])
```

This means that it does not copy the data from the sliced array to the new array but instead contains a view of the full array. Numpy does this to avoid memory problems when working with a huge array. To copy a certain slice of the array, we use the copy method off the slice we would like to copy. For example:

```
my_array = np.arange(0,10)

slice_array = my_array.copy()

my_array
array([0, 1, 2, 3, 4, 5, 6, 7, 8, 9])

slice_array
array([0, 1, 2, 3, 4, 5, 6, 7, 8, 9])
```

Now if we try to broadcast a value in the slice array, it will not affect the original array but only the copied values.

NumPy Arrays Operations

Numpy arrays support types of operations that include:

❖ Arithmetic Operations

❖ Conditional Expressions

❖ Logical Operations

1: Arithmetic Operations

NumPy arrays allow for basic arithmetic operations such as additions, subtractions, and such. However, if you add arrays with different number of elements and similar dimension, python will return an error.

```
array1 = np.array([10,20,30,40,50])
array2 = np.array([0, 1, 2, 3, 4])
array3 = array1 + array2
```

```
array3
```

```
array([10, 21, 32, 43, 54])
```

The result is an array of the same dimension.

Arithmetic operations with scalar value return an array with each action performed on each array element.

```
array2 = [10,20,30]
nd_array = np.array(array2)
nd_array*2
```

```
array([20, 40, 60])
```

These operations are also applicable to multi-dimensional arrays. Other mathematical functions discussed earlier can apply to numpy arrays too.

2: Conditional Expression

You can use python conditional statements to search the values matching specified conditions. The return value of conditional check on numpy array is an array of Boolean values.

```
bool_array = array1 < 10
```

```
bool_array
```

```
array([False, False, False, False, False])
```

You can also pass an array of Booleans to an array to return the values matching the condition.

3: Logical Operations

NumPy provides logical operator such as `logical_or` and `logical_and`. Numpy supports other functions such as reshape.

To find out more about numpy array operations, follow the link given below:

https://bit.ly/2oxeQ6Y

Pandas

Pandas is a data analysis, open source library built on NumPy, which is why we covered NumPy first. Pandas offer fast data analysis techniques, data cleaning, and data preparation. Compared to other data analysis libraries, pandas is very fast in terms of performance and productivity. It also offers built-in visualization features for quick graphical plotting of the data. Pandas also supports data from various external sources such as databases and spreadsheet programs.

Installing Pandas

We recommend using the anaconda distribution to avoid the hustle of installing these libraries. In case you prefer otherwise, open the command prompt or terminal, and enter the commands:

```
conda install Pandas

python -m pip install Pandas
```

In this section, we are going to cover the following Pandas features and discuss how they interact with data analysis:

❖ Pandas Series

❖ Pandas DataFrames

❖ Dealing with Missing Data

❖ GroupBy operations

❖ Concatenation, Merging and Joining DataFrames

❖ Pandas Operations

❖ Dealing with External data – Input and Output

Pandas Series

We can describe a Pandas series as a one-dimensional array object container that holds an array of data with labeled indexes. First, let us create several python objects as shown below:

```python
import numpy as np
import pandas as pd
```

```python
labels = ['A','B','C','D']
data = [100,200,300,400]
array = np.array(data)
my_dict = {"a":10,"b":20,"c":30,"d":40}
```

We import numpy as np and then Pandas as pd. We then create 4 python objects: a list called labels, another list called data, and a numpy array called array, and finally a dictionary called my_dict.

To create a Pandas series, we call the Pandas.series() function passing the data

```python
pd.Series(data = data)
```
```
0    100
1    200
2    300
3    400
dtype: int64
```

The output above looks like a NumPy array. However, the left shows indexes and the right shows the values. The Pandas.Series() function takes a number of parameters, of which one is the index. However, since we did not specify the index at which we want our data to start, the default index o applied automatically. If you want to specify the index to use for the Pandas series, you can pass the index as the second argument as shown below:

```
pd.Series(data=data,index=labels)
A    100
B    200
C    300
D    400
dtype: int64
```

This allocates the data with a specific identifier. This makes a Pandas series more efficient than the NumPy arrays since you can use values in the given indexes when selecting values.

If you take a python dictionary, Pandas will automatically convert the keys of the dictionary and make them the index of the series. If the data contained in a dictionary is not an integer, Pandas assigns it NaN value meaning Not a Number.

```
pd.Series(my_dict)
```

```
a    10
b    20
c    30
d    40
dtype: int64
```

You can also create a Pandas series from a numpy array that python treats as a python list. If you do not specify the labels, Pandas will automatically create labels as index from 0 upwards.

```
pd.Series(array)
```

```
0    100
1    200
2    300
3    400
dtype: int32
```

Pandas series can hold any python data type as the data. These include string or even python built-in functions. This shows that Pandas series is very flexible compared to NumPy array. However, if you use python functions as the actual data, pandas will hold their reference and not their default names. For example:

```
pd.Series(data=[sum,len,type,max])
0       <built-in function sum>
1       <built-in function len>
2                 <class 'type'>
3       <built-in function max>
dtype: object
```

In most cases, you will not find yourself storing references to python functions and classes – this is just to illustrate the flexibility of the Pandas Series.

Let us go ahead and illustrate how to grab information from a pandas series.

```
In [7]:  series1 = pd.Series([2000,3000,4000],['CA','OR','UT'])

In [8]:  series1

Out[8]:  CA    2000
         OR    3000
         UT    4000
         dtype: int64
```

Fetching information from a pandas series is very similar to python dictionaries. However, instead of passing keys as the value, we pass the index name or number. For example, to get the information of the state OR, we pass:

```
series1["OR"]
```

```
3000
```

If the indexes of the series are strings, you pass the string as the value and an integer if the indexes are numbers. In most cases, the index will be a number or a string.

NumPy operations do not affect the index of the data. If you operate on a Pandas series such as math operations or multiplication by a scalar value, it will not alter the index.

```
series1 * 2
```

```
CA     4000
OR     6000
UT     8000
dtype: int64
```

This only affects the data, which ensures preservation of the index of the data. If you perform a certain operation on two data types such as addition, it will convert the data into a float in order not to lose the accuracy of the data due to some weird mathematical operation.

Pandas DataFrames

Pandas DataFrames are tabular representation of two-dimensional data with labeled rows and columns. It is more like a spreadsheet. There are several ways to construct a pandas DataFrame. You can create DataFrame by passing a list, dictionaries, and even arrays.

Open the Jupyter notebook and import numpy as np and pandas as pd. Also, import the randn from numpy.random

```
import numpy as np
import pandas as pd
from numpy.random import randn
```

To create a Pandas DataFrame, we use the DataFrame () function like the Series () function as shown below:

```
DataFrame = pd.DataFrame(randn(6,5),['A','B','C','D','E','F'],['P','Q','R','S','T'])
```

DataFrame

	P	Q	R	S	T
A	0.937082	0.731000	1.361556	-0.326238	0.055676
B	0.222400	-1.443217	0.756352	0.816454	0.750445
C	-0.455947	1.189622	-1.690617	-1.356399	-1.232435
D	-0.544439	-0.668172	0.007315	-0.612939	1.299748
E	-1.733096	-0.983310	0.357508	-1.613579	1.470714
F	-1.188018	-0.549746	-0.940046	-0.827932	0.108863

The first arguments generates random data using the rand method, the second argument indicates the corresponding rows, while the third represent the number of columns. Pandas series are like Excel spreadsheets. However, each of

81

the columns in a pandas DataFrame is itself a pandas series. For example:

```
DataFrame['P']
```

```
A     0.937082
B     0.222400
C    -0.455947
D    -0.544439
E    -1.733096
F    -1.188018
Name: P, dtype: float64
```

```
DataFrame['Q']
```

```
A     0.731000
B    -1.443217
C     1.189622
D    -0.668172
E    -0.983310
F    -0.549746
Name: Q, dtype: float64
```

You can see that the column P itself contains a pandas series with its own independent index labels. In other words, a DataFrame is a bunch of Pandas Series that share a common index. You can confirm this by passing it to the type function.

```
type(DataFrame['Q'])
```

```
pandas.core.series.Series
```

The best way to select columns in a pandas DataFrame is by passing the index notation. However, if you are familiar with SQL, you can pass the column similar to SQL table fetch using:

```
DataFrame.P
A     0.937082
B     0.222400
C    -0.455947
D    -0.544439
E    -1.733096
F    -1.188018
Name: P, dtype: float64
```

NOTE: This method is not ideal as it may end up over writing the default pandas DataFrame methods. This will confuse pandas whether you are enquiring for a column name or a Method.

However, despite a single column being a pandas series, if you call for two or more columns, the result will be a DataFrame by itself.

```
DataFrame[['P','S']]
```

	P	S
A	0.937082	-0.326238
B	0.222400	0.816454
C	-0.455947	-1.356399
D	-0.544439	-0.612939
E	-1.733096	-1.613579
F	-1.188018	-0.827932

```
type(DataFrame[['P','S']])
```
```
pandas.core.frame.DataFrame
```

To create a new column, we can call it as if it already exists as long as we pass the value we want assigned to it. For example, if we create a column called "sum" and assign the value as sum of column P and Q:

```
DataFrame['SUM'] = DataFrame['P'] + DataFrame['Q']
```
```
DataFrame
```

	P	Q	R	S	T	SUM
A	0.937082	0.731000	1.361556	-0.326238	0.055676	1.668083
B	0.222400	-1.443217	-0.756352	0.816454	0.750445	-1.220817
C	-0.455947	1.189622	-1.690617	-1.356399	-1.232435	0.733675
D	-0.544439	-0.668172	0.007315	-0.612939	1.299748	-1.212611
E	-1.733096	-0.983310	0.357508	-1.613579	1.470714	-2.716406
F	-1.188018	-0.549746	-0.940046	-0.827932	0.108863	-1.737764

To delete a column, you can use the .drop method – as we do in SQL programming.

```
DataFrame.drop('R', axis=1)
```

	P	Q	S	T	SUM
A	0.937082	0.731000	-0.326238	0.055676	1.668083
B	0.222400	-1.443217	0.816454	0.750445	-1.220817
C	-0.455947	1.189622	-1.356399	-1.232435	0.733675
D	-0.544439	-0.668172	-0.612939	1.299748	-1.212611

If you call the drop method without passing axis=1, it will result in an error. This is because by default, the axis is set to 0 which refers to the index of the DataFrame.

When using the drop method, the changes do not occur in place of the original data frame. For example, if we look at the data frame after the drop method, it will retain the original values unless specified otherwise.

```
DataFrame
```

	P	Q	R	S	T	SUM
A	-1.749765	0.342680	1.153036	-0.252436	0.981321	-1.407085
B	0.514219	0.221180	-1.070043	-0.189496	0.255001	0.735399
C	-0.458027	0.435163	-0.583595	0.816847	0.672721	-0.022863
D	-0.104411	-0.531280	1.029733	-0.438136	-1.118318	-0.635692
E	1.618982	1.541605	-0.251879	-0.842436	0.184519	3.160587
F	0.937082	0.731000	1.361556	-0.326238	0.055676	1.668083

To make the changes permanent to the original data frame, we specify the Inplace argument to true as shown below:

```
DataFrame.drop('R',axis=1,inplace=True)
```

```
DataFrame
```

	P	Q	S	T	SUM
A	-1.749765	0.342680	-0.252436	0.981321	-1.407085
B	0.514219	0.221180	-0.189496	0.255001	0.735399
C	-0.458027	0.435163	0.816847	0.672721	-0.022863
D	-0.104411	-0.531280	-0.438136	-1.118318	-0.635692
E	1.618982	1.541605	-0.842436	0.184519	3.160587
F	0.937082	0.731000	-0.326238	0.055676	1.668083

Most of pandas methods will require that you set the inplace argument to true. This ensures that you do not accidentally lose data. You can also use the drop method to delete both rows and columns as long as the axis specified for the operation matches the specified value.

If you are wondering about the reason why rows are at 0 axis and the columns at 1 axis, the reason behind it is Numpy arrays. If you call the shape of the data frame, it will return a tuple as a two-dimensional matrix as shown below:

```
DataFrame.shape
```

```
(6, 5)
```

The index 0 element in the tuple represents the number of rows while the index 1 value in the tuple represents the number of columns. Thus, 0 is rows and 1 is columns

The difference comes in when selecting rows and columns in a data frame. To select columns, you can pass a label for the column or a list of column labels. On the other hand, to select rows, we use the .loc and the .iloc method. These two methods use square brackets instead of the usual parenthesis.

```
DataFrame.loc['A']
P       -1.749765
Q        0.342680
S       -0.252436
T        0.981321
SUM     -1.407085
Name: A, dtype: float64
```

The result of a single row and a single column is the same as it returns a pandas series.

The .iloc method allows us to grab rows using the numerical index even if the rows labels are in strings. For example:

```
DataFrame.iloc[2]
P      -0.458027
Q       0.435163
S       0.816847
T       0.672721
SUM    -0.022863
Name: C, dtype: float64
```

This shows that labeling of the loc method depends on location while the iloc is a numerical index based location.

To select subsets of rows and columns, we just specify the row and column required. For example, if we want to grab the element at row A and column S, we call the loc method as shown:

```
DataFrame.loc['A','S']

-0.25243603652138985
```

Let use move on to discussing conditional selection using the Pandas DataFrame.

The conditional selection for pandas DataFrames is very similar to that of Numpy. For example, if you use a conditional check against a DataFrame of values greater than 1, you will get a data frame of Boolean values as shown below:

```
DataFrame > 1
```

	P	Q	S	T	SUM
A	False	False	False	False	False
B	False	False	False	False	False
C	False	False	False	False	False
D	False	False	False	False	False
E	True	True	False	False	True
F	False	False	False	False	True

If you save the result of the above conditional check to variable and check it against the original data frame, it will result with values where it was true and NaN where the condition happened to be false:

```
DataFrame[Boolean_DataFrame]
```

	P	Q	S	T	SUM
A	NaN	NaN	NaN	NaN	NaN
B	NaN	NaN	NaN	NaN	NaN
C	NaN	NaN	NaN	NaN	NaN
D	NaN	NaN	NaN	NaN	NaN
E	1.618982	1.541605	NaN	NaN	3.160587
F	NaN	NaN	NaN	NaN	1.668083

For this case, the values greater than 1 were less than the values greater than one, which resulted in a large number of NaN values.

This operation of using an entire data frame against a conditional operation is not very common. The more common way is just to call the row or column against a conditional operation.

```
DataFrame[DataFrame['P']>0]
```

	P	Q	S	T	SUM
B	0.514219	0.221180	-0.189496	0.255001	0.735399
E	1.618982	1.541605	-0.842436	0.184519	3.160587
F	0.937082	0.731000	-0.326238	0.055676	1.668083

This will result in a data frame where only the values greater than 0 are shown. This conditional operation is very useful while performing filter operations against a specific column or in rare cases, an entire DataFrame

So far, we have only dealt with single condition based off a column or row. If we want to combine multiple conditions, we can use the brackets and the logical operators to perform this operation.

```
DataFrame[(DataFrame['P']>0) & (DataFrame['Q'])]
```

	P	Q	S	T	SUM
B	0.514219	0.221180	-0.189496	0.255001	0.735399
E	1.618982	1.541605	-0.842436	0.184519	3.160587
F	0.937082	0.731000	-0.326238	0.055676	1.668083

However, you may notice that we used the ampersand instead of the normal python and operator. This is because the **and operator** cannot work with a series of Boolean values. If you pass a series of Boolean values, it gets confused and results in an error about the data being ambiguous as shown below:

```
DataFrame[(DataFrame['P']>0) and (DataFrame['Q'])]

--------------------------------------------------------------
ValueError                         Traceback (most recent call last)
<ipython-input-24-d12b623803f4> in <module>
----> 1 DataFrame[(DataFrame['P']>0) and (DataFrame['Q'])]

C:\ProgramData\Anaconda3\lib\site-packages\pandas\core\generic.py in __nonzero__(self)
   1476         raise ValueError("The truth value of a {0} is ambiguous. "
   1477                          "Use a.empty, a.bool(), a.item(), a.any() or a.all()."
-> 1478                          .format(self.__class__.__name__))
   1479
   1480     __bool__ = __nonzero__

ValueError: The truth value of a Series is ambiguous. Use a.empty, a.bool(), a.item(), a.any() or a.all().
```

Similarly, the normal python OR operator is replaced with the pipe operator |

If we want to reset the indexes of a data frame to the default ones – i.e. 0, 1, 2, 3, 4...nth row, We call the .reset_index() method as shown below

DataFrame

	P	Q	S	T	SUM
A	-1.749765	0.342680	-0.252436	0.981321	-1.407085
B	0.514219	0.221180	-0.189496	0.255001	0.735399
C	-0.458027	0.435163	0.816847	0.672721	-0.022863
D	-0.104411	-0.531280	-0.438136	-1.118318	-0.635692
E	1.618982	1.541605	-0.842436	0.184519	3.160587
F	0.937082	0.731000	-0.326238	0.055676	1.668083

DataFrame.reset_index()

	index	P	Q	S	T	SUM
0	A	-1.749765	0.342680	-0.252436	0.981321	-1.407085
1	B	0.514219	0.221180	-0.189496	0.255001	0.735399
2	C	-0.458027	0.435163	0.816847	0.672721	-0.022863
3	D	-0.104411	-0.531280	-0.438136	-1.118318	-0.635692
4	E	1.618982	1.541605	-0.842436	0.184519	3.160587
5	F	0.937082	0.731000	-0.326238	0.055676	1.668083

However, this does not delete the current index but it instead pushes it to become a column in the data frame called index.

DATA SCIENCE WITH PYTHON

Like other pandas methods, this change does not occur inline and the original data frame remains the same. To make the changes permanent, we set the inline attribute to True.

To set a column in the data frame as the index, we use the set_index method off the data frame. For example, let us have a column with states abbreviation as:

```
indexs = 'NY, OR, UT, WY, CA, TX'.split()
```

```
indexs
```

```
['NY,', 'OR,', 'UT,', 'WY,', 'CA,', 'TX']
```

```
DataFrame['States'] = indexs
```

```
DataFrame
```

index		P	Q	S	T	SUM	States
0	A	-1.749765	0.342680	-0.252436	0.981321	-1.407085	NY,
1	B	0.514219	0.221180	-0.189496	0.255001	0.735399	OR,
2	C	-0.458027	0.435163	0.816847	0.672721	-0.022863	UT,
3	D	-0.104411	-0.531280	-0.438136	-1.118318	-0.635692	WY,
4	E	1.618982	1.541605	-0.842436	0.184519	3.160587	CA,
5	F	0.937082	0.731000	-0.326238	0.055676	1.668083	TX

```
DataFrame.set_index('States')
```

States	index	P	Q	S	T	SUM
NY,	A	-1.749765	0.342680	-0.252436	0.981321	-1.407085
OR,	B	0.514219	0.221180	-0.189496	0.255001	0.735399
UT,	C	-0.458027	0.435163	0.816847	0.672721	-0.022863
WY,	D	-0.104411	-0.531280	-0.438136	-1.118318	-0.635692
CA,	E	1.618982	1.541605	-0.842436	0.184519	3.160587
TX	F	0.937082	0.731000	-0.326238	0.055676	1.668083

1: Input And Ouput Data

As a library, Pandas can read and write data to a wide variety of sources and formats. In this part, we are going to focus on mainly four data sources and formats. They include csv files, spreadsheet programs, HTML files, and SQL data sources.

In order to work with some of these formats, pandas will need to install several libraries. Enter the commands below to install the required packages:

```
conda install sqlalchemy
```

```
conda install lxml
```

```
conda install beautifulsoup4
```

94

```
conda install html5lib
```

NOTE: You can replace the Conda with pip to install these packages. Some of these packages may not be on your system by default even if you are using the Anaconda distribution.

Open the Jupyter notebook to start reading and writing files. In order to read files, you need to make sure that the Jupyter notebook is in the same location as the file you are trying to read. To check the current location of Jupyter notebook, enter the command:

```
import pandas as pd
```

```
pwd
```

```
'C:\\Users\\capta'
```

To read a csv file, enter the command pd.read_csv("full-csv-filename") as shown below:

```
pd.read_csv("10000 Sales Records.csv")
```

	Region	Country	Item Type	Sales Channel	Order Priority	Order Date	Order ID	Ship Date	Units Sold	Unit Price	Unit Cost	Total Revenue	Total Cost	Total Profit
0	Sub-Saharan Africa	Chad	Office Supplies	Online	L	1/27/2011	292494523	2/12/2011	4484	651.21	524.96	2920025.64	2353920.64	566105.00
1	Europe	Latvia	Beverages	Online	C	12/28/2015	361825549	1/23/2016	1075	47.45	31.79	51008.75	34174.25	16834.50
2	Middle East and North Africa	Pakistan	Vegetables	Offline	C	1/13/2011	141515767	2/1/2011	6515	154.06	90.93	1003700.90	592408.95	411291.95
3	Sub-Saharan Africa	Democratic Republic of the Congo	Household	Online	C	9/11/2012	500364005	10/6/2012	7683	668.27	502.54	5134318.41	3861014.82	1273303.59
4	Europe	Czech Republic	Beverages	Online	C	10/27/2015	127481591	12/5/2015	3491	47.45	31.79	165647.95	110978.89	54669.06

To get the sample data used in this book and for practice purposes, use the following link to download an entire zip file of data sources.

https://bit.ly/2nSpAwK

Pandas offers a wide variety of ways to read data such html, json, sql, hmtl, clipboard, etc.

You can also write data to a csv file. For this, you need to specify the data frame to use followed by the name of the output.

```
my_dataframe = pd.read_csv("10000 Sales Records.csv")
```

```
my_dataframe.to_csv("my_dataframe",index=False)
```

From the above example, we read the previous csv saved to a data frame called my_dataframe, we then save the data frame into a csv file called my_dataframe.csv. Specifying the index to False removes the index instead of creating a column called unknown as shown:

```
pd.read_csv("my_dataframe")
```

	Unnamed: 0	Region	Country	Item Type	Sales Channel	Order Priority
0	0	Sub-Saharan Africa	Chad	Office Supplies	Online	L
1	1	Europe	Latvia	Beverages	Online	C
2	2	Middle East and North	Pakistan	Vegetables	Offline	C

You can also output the data frame into various formats as you can read them. These formats include copy to clipboard, csv, json, txt, hmtl, sql etc.

For the case of excel files such as .Xsls, pandas can only read the data but cannot import images, formulas, and macros. Do not use pd.read_excel with such type of data as it may lead pandas to crash and lose data. When reading data from excel files containing more than workbook, it creates data frames where each data frame is every workbook within the file.

When it comes to SQL files, Pandas is not suited to reading this kind of data since there are many flavors of SQL engines such as PostgreSQL, MySQL, Oracle, Microsoft SQL Server, SQLite etc. Depending on the Engine you are using, specific drivers, and libraries are more developed towards that engine and you may require to do some research to find the best library and package.

To illustrate how to read data from SQL tables, we are going to create a simple SQL engine held up in the memory.

Once we import the create_engine module, we are going to create a postgresql engine for test purposes. You can also use MySQL or SQLite but ensure you have the dependencies installed. If you wish to use PostgreSQL, use the following command to install a driver called psycopg2

```
conda install pyscopg2
```

```
from sqlalchemy import create_engine
from sqlalchemy.dialects import postgresql
```

```
engine = create_engine("postgresql:///:memory:")
```

```
my_dataframe.to_sql('sample_table',con=engine)
```

NOTE: If you try to use an engine not installed, you will get an error.

Connecting with databases is very challenging for beginners. To get more information about how SQLalchemy works:

https://bit.ly/2mW3GIJ

2: Missing Data In Pandas

Cases of missing data are especially common while working with external data. Although we usually clean and recheck data from sources such as Kaggle, data from sources such as logs and spreadsheets may have some missing data. If pandas encounters missing data, it automatically assigns the value Not a Number value (NaN). In real world cases, Missing data is very problematic and can cause inaccurate results.

Fortunately, pandas provide functions that allow us to check for missing within the specified DataFrame. These functions are `isnull()` and `notnull()`

These two functions return a Boolean value where the two cases are true or false. In cases where you have missing data, you can manually fill in the data or use Pandas built in functions to generate random but similar data.

Functions such as `replace()`, `fillna()` or `interpolate()` and `dropna()` provide the ability to delete or fill the missing data within the data frame. This saves lots of time compared to manually entering the data and dealing with the errors that may occur due to missing data.

We use the `dropna()` function to remove the rows and columns that have missing data in the DataFrame. The table below shows the most common Pandas DataFrame methods.

DataFrame Function	Function Operation
isnull()	Checks for missing values in a DataFrame and returns Boolean true for true cases
notnull()	Checks for missing values and returns false where there is no missing data

where()	Check DataFrame for a given condition
rename()	Used to rename indexes of columns and rows in a DataFrame
fillna()	Allows user to specify the filling value for missing data
copy()	Creates a copy of Pandas objects

drop_duplicates	Filters and removes duplicates in a pandas DataFrame
set_index()	Used to set index of DataFrame rows
reset_index()	Resets the indexes in a pandas DataFrame
insert()	Inserts new columns in a DataFrame

values()	Returns a DataFrame without axes and labels —it's more like a NumPy array

3: Pandas GroupBy

The pandas GroupBy function allows you to group rows together and call aggregate functions. The GroupBy function in pandas works in similar ways as in SQL programming.

Let us assume you have three partitions of data as shown

ID	VALUE
1	50.30
1	123.30
1	132.90
2	50.30
2	123.30
2	132.90

2	88.90
3	50.30
3	123.30

Each ID represents each partition. You can group them using the ID column and perform some aggregate function. An aggregate function is any function that accepts two or more values and returns one value. The statistical mean function is an example of an aggregate function.

Let us look at how to perform GroupBy operations in pandas. First, let us create a sample data as shown below:

```
data = {'Company':['GOOGLE', 'GOOGLE','MICROSOFT','MICROSOFT','FACEBOOK','FACEBOOK'],
        'CEO':['SAM','CHARLIE','AMY','HOWARD','SARAH','MICHAEL'],
        'INCOME':[200,220,340,224,243,350]}
```

Once you have entered the data above, convert it to a pandas DataFrame.

```
dataFrame = pd.DataFrame(data)
```

Now you can use the GroupBy method to group rows together based off a column name. Let us group by the company names.

```
sort_by_company = dataFrame.groupby('Company')
```

The above code provides you a pandas DataFrame group by object. Save it as a variable.

Now you can call the aggregate function on the GroupBy object provided. Let us call the mean off this object.

```
sort_by_company.mean()
```

Company	INCOME
FACEBOOK	296.5
GOOGLE	210.0
MICROSOFT	282.0

This results to the mcan values based on the company. However, it cannot return a mean off the names since they are strings and cannot perform aggregate functions on non-numerical values.

Section 7: Data Visualization With Matplotlib And Seaborn

Data visualization is the graphical analysis and interpretation of scientific data. The aim of data visualization is to make better decisions. In python, data visualization involves using scientific libraries and packages to represent data visually for better interpretation.

Here are the most important elements you need to have in mind when working with Python for data visualization

Matplotlib

From the official Matplotlib website:

"Matplotlib is a Python 2D plotting library that produces publication quality figures in a variety of hardcopy formats and interactive environments across platforms."

Matplotlib is a python-plotting library that allows you to create visual representations of data such as graphs, heat maps, and more in 2D. Matplotlib has the same MATLAB graphical capabilities and provides complete control of the figures plotted.

Matplotlib works efficiently with pandas DataFrames and NumPy Arrays and is acts as a foundation for another plotting library we will learn about later called Seaborn, which means to learn Seaborn, we must first understand how Matplotlib works.

Installing Matplotlib

As usual, if you are using the Anaconda distribution, chances are you have Matplotlib pre-installed already. In case you are using another python installation, you can install it by inputting the following command:

```
conda install matplotlib

pip install matplotlib
```

To use Matplotlib, we need to import it along with other relevant libraries, which you can do as follows:

```
import pandas as pd
import numpy as np
from matplotlib import pyplot as plt
```

Let us first create two NumPy arrays that are linearly spaced using the linspace function. Matplotlib offers two ways to create plots, i.e., the functional method and the object-oriented method. We will cover the functional way now and later shift to the Object Oriented r.

```
x = np.linspace(0,5,11)
y = x ** 2
```

The basic way to perform a plot in matplotlib is to call the plot function and pass the arguments to plot against.

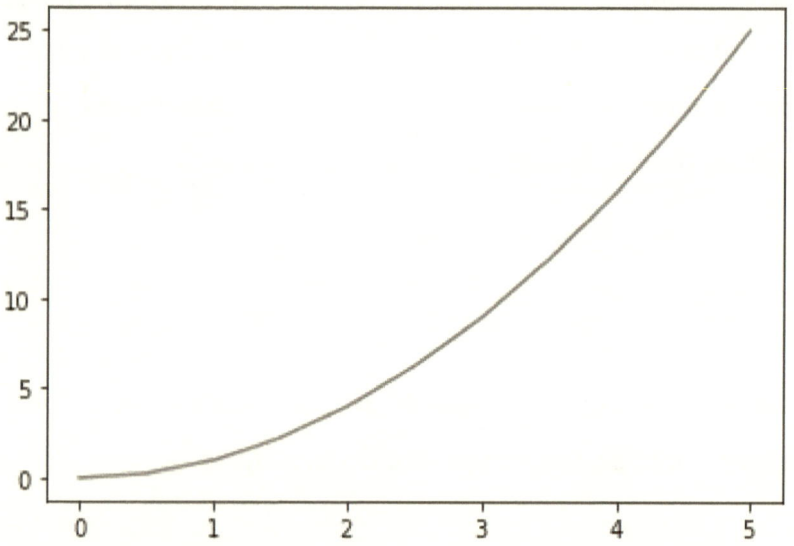

This plots x against y as shown above. Matplotlib plots take arguments similar to the MATLAB arguments such as color and line format. Other useful methods for Matplotlib are available allowing us to add titles and x and y labels.

To add a y label, we pass the xlabel method with the label name as a string argument. The same case to the y label and the title of the plot.

```
plt.plot(x,y)
plt.xlabel("X Values")
plt.ylabel("Y Values")
plt.title("Plot of X and Y")
```

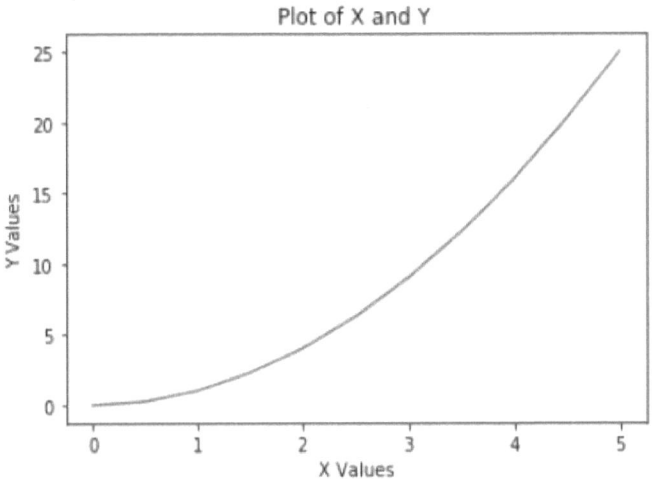

Matplotlib allows you to have different representations of the same data. The following are some of the supported Matplotlib representation.

❖ Bar graphs

❖ Scatter plots

❖ Histograms

You can use the following functions to plot your desired representation.

1: Bar Graphs

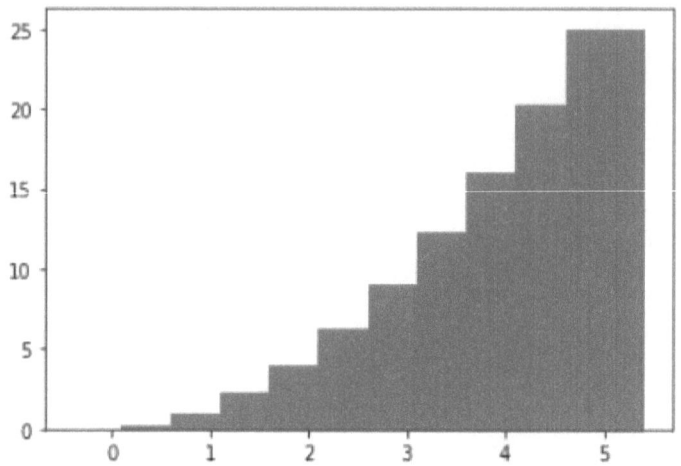

We will use the above data to plot the representations.
```
plt.bar(X, Y)
```

2: Scatter Plots

```
plt.scatter(X,Y)
```

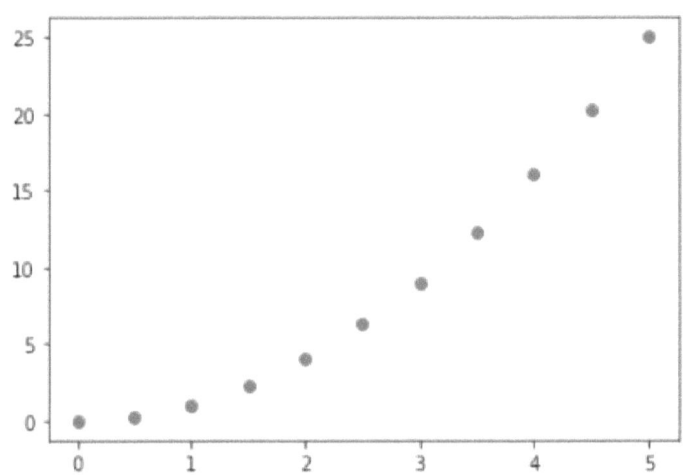

3: Histograms

```
plt.hist(Y)
```

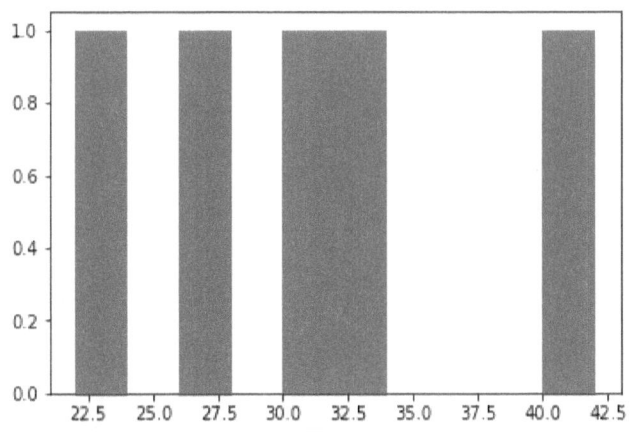

Matplotlib is a very advanced scientific plotting library. To learn more about the Matplotlib plotting capabilities, navigate to the following invaluable resource page:

https://matplotlib.org/index.html

Seaborn

Seaborn is the most popular statistical plotting python library built on top of Matplotlib. Compared to other python plotting libraries, Seaborn has more beautiful and detailed styles. Seaborn supports and works efficiently on pandas DataFrame Objects.

Installing Seaborn

Just like all the other libraries we have used previously, Seaborn comes pre-packaged in the Anaconda distribution. If you are not using the Anaconda distro, you can install it using the following command:

```
conda install seaborn
```

```
pip install seaborn
```

Seaborn is Github-hosted but contains very organized gallery and documentation found on the link below.

https://seaborn.pydata.org/

In this section, we are going to discuss the following plots provided by seaborn.

- ❖ Distribution Plots

- ❖ Joint plots

- ❖ Categorical Plots

- ❖ Matrix Plots

- ❖ Colors and Styles

- ❖ Regression Plots

- ❖ Seaborn Grids

Distribution Plots

We are going to look at some of Seaborn plots that allow us to visualize the distribution of a data set. These plots are going to show detailed distribution patterns of a certain data set.

First, let us import Seaborn as sns as this is the conventional way of doing so.

```
import seaborn as sns
```

We are going to use the built-in seaborn datasets for this illustration. Load the data using the following code:

```
import seaborn as sns
```

```
my_data = sns.load_dataset('tips')
```

```
my_data.head()
```

	total_bill	tip	sex	smoker	day	time	size
0	16.99	1.01	Female	No	Sun	Dinner	2
1	10.34	1.66	Male	No	Sun	Dinner	3
2	21.01	3.50	Male	No	Sun	Dinner	3
3	23.68	3.31	Male	No	Sun	Dinner	2
4	24.59	3.61	Female	No	Sun	Dinner	4

Distribution plots allow you to view the distribution of a single variable. To create a distribution plot, use this command:

```
sns.distplot(data['total_bill'])
```

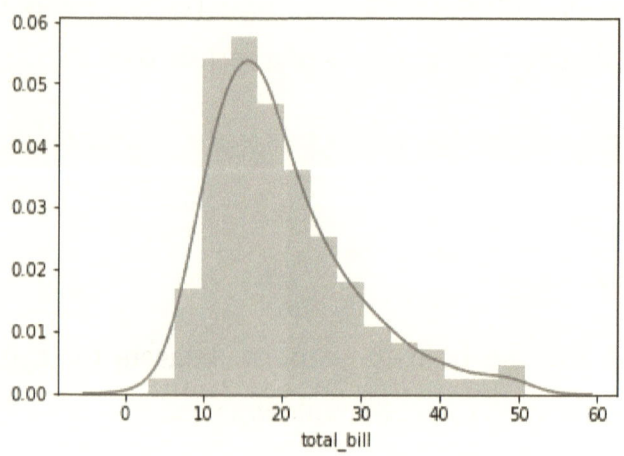

If you are using the tips dataset, you should get an almost similar plot. Some versions of the anaconda distribution will produce an error about the statsmodel library. Ignore this error.

The above plots show a histogram and a KDE plot—Kernel Density Estimation plot—that show the distribution of data over constant interval of time. You can remove it by passing the `kde=False in the distplot()` function.

To get a clearer representation of your data, you can add a `bins=number_of_bins` argument in the function. This produces a similar figure, only more detailed.

```
sns.distplot(data['total_bill'],kde=False,
bins=30)
```

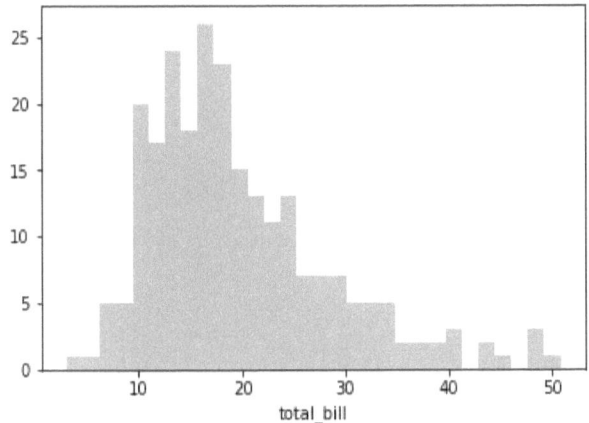

NOTE: Do not use a large bin value; otherwise, you will get a weird looking illustration with altered meaning.

1: Seaborn Joint Plots

Seaborn joint plots allow you to plot two distribution plots and compare data. To plot joint plots, you need to provide three main arguments; the x, y, and the data, which are column names of the dataset and the name of the data set:

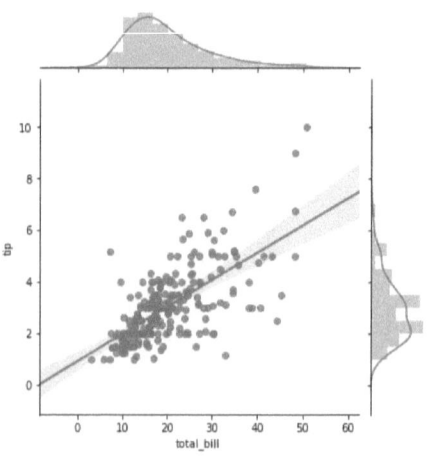

```
sns.jointplot(x='total_bill',          y='tip',
data=data, kind='reg')
```

Where x = 'column_name_one'

y = 'column_name_two'

data = 'dataset_name'

```
kind = 'type_of_plot'
```

We used the kind parameter to affect the type joint plot shown. You can set it to be a hist for histogram, reg for a scatter plot with a regression line, or a swarm.

2: Seaborn Pairplots

In Seaborn, we use Pairplots to plot pairwise relationships across entire DataFrame for numerical columns. To plot a Pairplot against a dataset, just pass the name of the dataset as follows:

```
sns.pairplot(data)
```

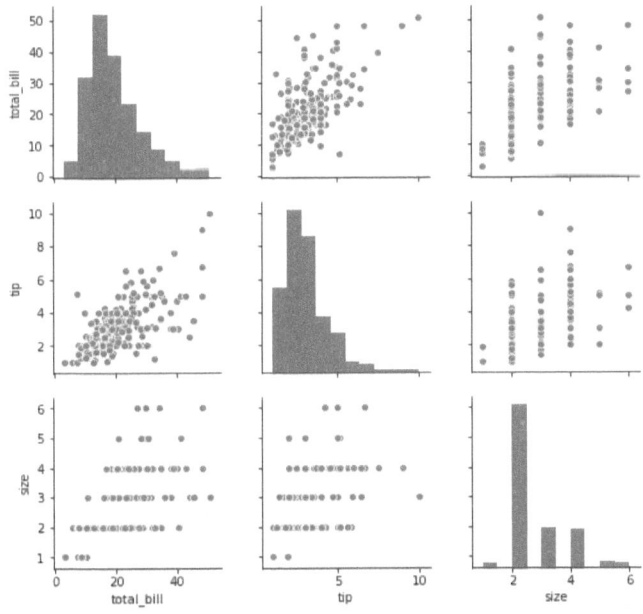

Pairplots represents visual data of the columns against another. In most cases, representation of a column against a column is in the form of a histogram instead of scatterplot as shown above. You can also add in a hue parameter, which is mostly a categorical column of the data. For example, in the dataset above, the column sex is categorical as there are only two categories in it. Such parameters provide an illustration such as the one shown below:

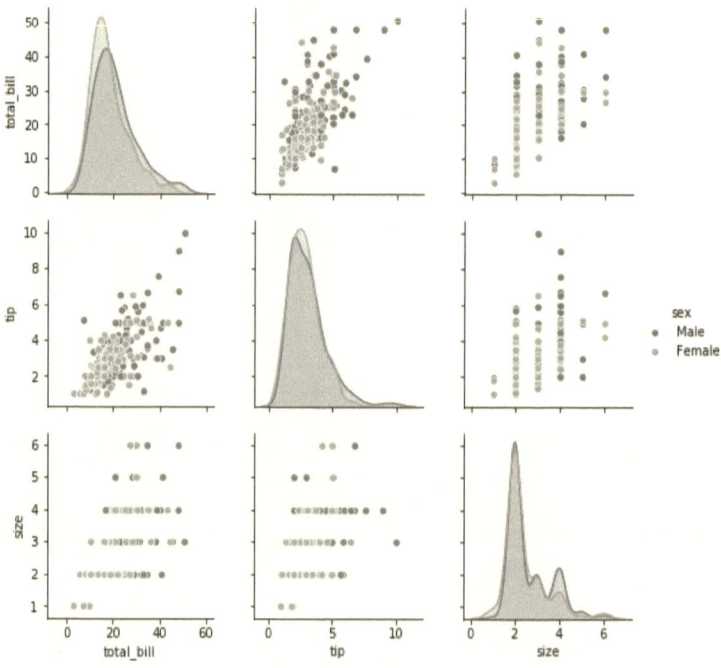

The above illustration indicates that Pairplots are a very effective way to visualize your data quickly.

Categorical Plots

Seaborn categorical plots allow you to plot categorical variables of nominal variables. Nominal variables are variables with two or more categories but have no order in the categories. We are going to work with the 'tips' dataset provided by Seaborn. Go ahead and load the dataset as above.

1: Seaborn Bar Plots

Bar plot, which is a very common type of plot, is just a general plot that allows you to aggregate categorical data off a specified function.

```
sns.barplot(x=, y=, data=) Which in this the
mean function.
```

Where x is the categorical column and y is a numerical column.

A plot like this shows the following:

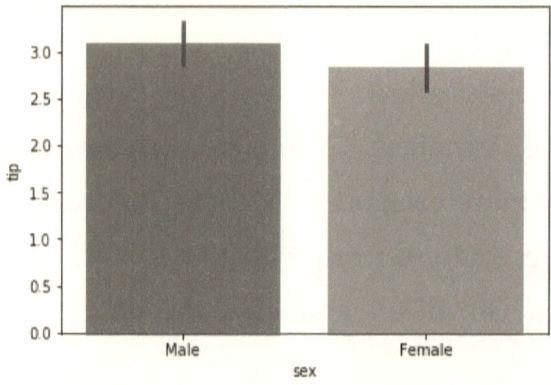

```
sns.barplot(x='sex', y='tip', data=data)
```

The above bar plot shows the mean of the 'tip' against categorical value 'sex' showing that the mean tip for Male is higher than that of Female. You can also provide an estimator parameter that is just a statistical function to use as an estimator for each categorical bin, which by default is the mean. An example would be a standard deviation of the tip per gender.

To find the standard deviation of the two data, you can use the numpy std function as shown below:

```
sns.barplot(x='sex', y='tip', data=data,
estimator=np.std)
```

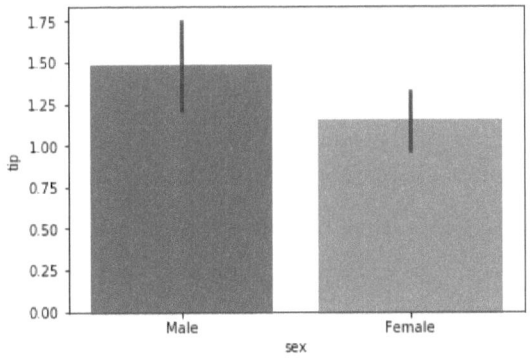

This just shows the standard deviation of 'tip' against each gender. You can provide any statistical function you want whether built-in or custom created.

2: Seaborn Count Plots

In Seaborn, a count plot is like a bar plot except the estimator explicitly counts the number of occurrences. This means the arguments are like bar plot except the y-axis is already chosen thus only x and data parameters are passed.

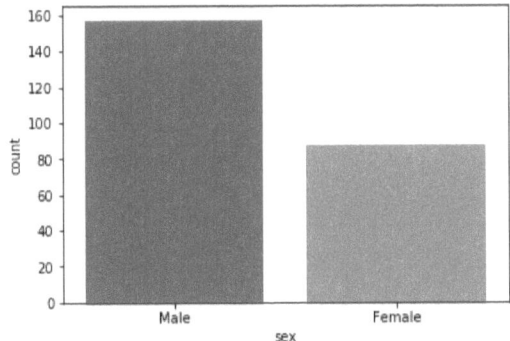

```
sns.countplot(x='sex', data=data)
```

3: Seaborn Box Plots

We use these two types of plots to represent the distribution of categorical data graphically. Also called whisker plot, Box plot shows the distribution of quantitate data in a method that helps with comparison of variables.

To create a box plot, you need to pass in a categorical data point (such as 'sex' or 'smoker' in the above data) as x, numerical data as y, and lastly, the dataset name as data:

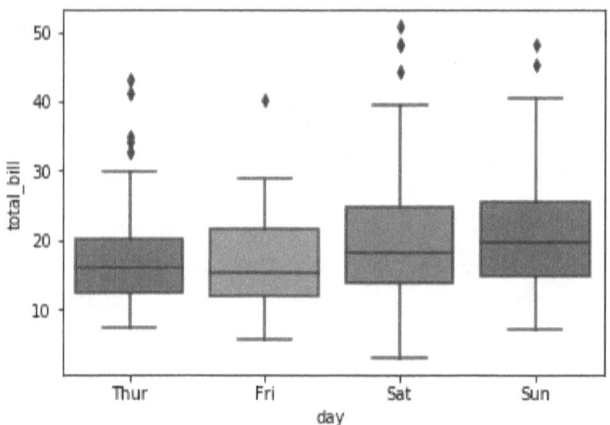

The above plot is from

```
sns.boxplot(x='day',            y='total_bill',
data=data)
```

The box plot shows the quartile of the dataset while the whiskers show the rest of the distribution. Seaborn allows you to add a hue parameter that should be a categorical data as well. For example, if you set hue to be smoker, you can be able to compare total bill by day and if the individual is a smoker.

4: Seaborn Violin plots

Violin plots are like box plots with parameters x, y, and data. Unlike box plots, violin plots let you plot all components that match with actual data points. We create a violin plot by calling the:

```
sns.violinplot(params)
```

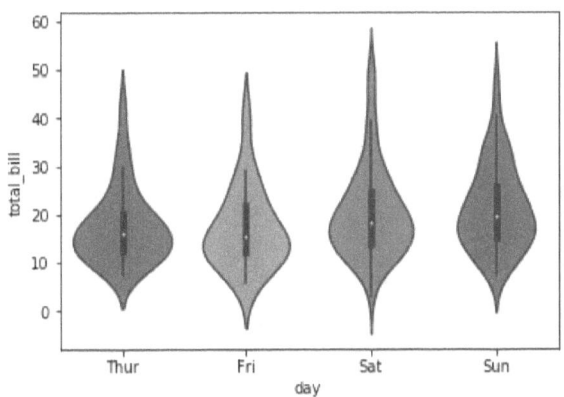

```
sns.violinplot(x='day',y='total_bill',data=da
ta)
```

In regards to data points, Violin plots are more detailed. The only disadvantage to using violin plots —as opposed to box plots— is that violin plots are very difficult to interpret. Like a boxplot, a violin plot accepts hue parameters. You can also provide the split parameter, which accepts a Boolean value, to split the distributions of other categories. For example,

```
sns.violinplot(x='day',y='total_bill',data=da
ta, split=True)
```

5: Seaborn strip Plots

We use a Seaborn strip plot to represent univariate data, which means one variable. In Seaborn, a strip plot will plot a scatterplot where one variable is categorical and the other is numerical.

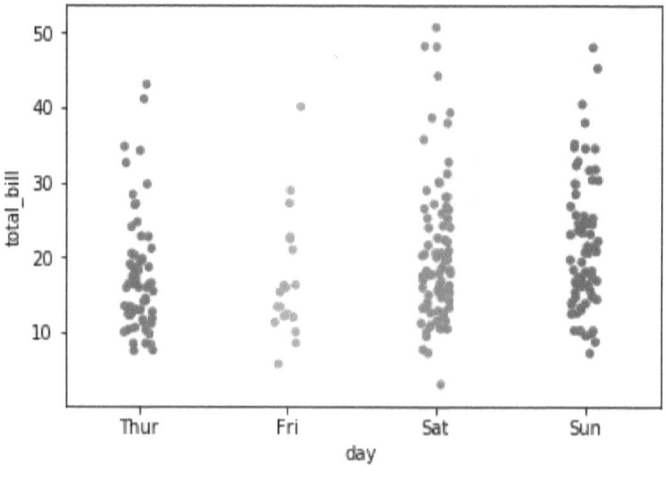

The above plot is of days against total bill using:

```
sns.stripplot(x='day',           y='total_bill',
data=data)
```

Compared to the visual appearance, Interpretation of stripplots is more difficult since you cannot tell which points stack on top of each other. Despite the fact, stripplots provide a method to add random noise to your dataset to try to make it more readable; it does not provide good interpretation.

```
sns.stripplot(x='day',           y='total_bill',
data=data, jitter=True)
```

6: Swarmplots

A swarm plot is a more readable version of a violin plot. Swarm plots adjust the points of the plot so that they do not overlap against each other thus providing more clear information of the distribution. It is more like combining a scatter plot with a violin plot:

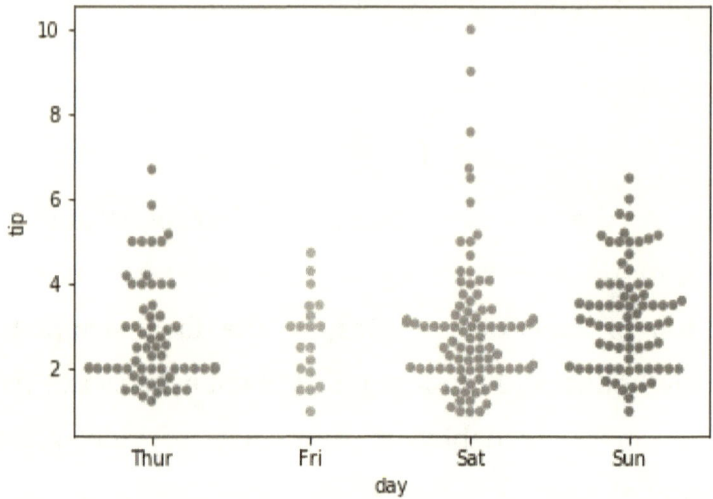

Despite being prettier and providing more information, the drawback to Swarmplots is that they do not work well with a very large dataset, which is usually the case with real world scenarios and applications.

Matrix Plots

Matrix plots are a series of scatter plots or an array of scatter plots. We shall cover how to create matrix plots and more specific, heat maps.

Type the following codes in Jupyter notebook.

```
import seaborn as sns
get_ipython().run_line_magic('matplotlib', 'inline')
tips_data = sns.load_dataset('tips')
flights_data = sns.load_dataset('flights')
tips_data.head()
flights_data.head()
```

	year	month	passengers
0	1949	January	112
1	1949	February	118
2	1949	March	132
3	1949	April	129
4	1949	May	121

From the above code, we loaded two datasets, i.e., tips and flights.

1: Heatmaps

Heatmaps are the primary way of showing matrix plots. For a heatmap to work correctly, the provided data should be in matrix form. This means the index name and columns value match that cell value.

If you look at the head of the above data, for example tips_data, you will notice that it is not in matrix format. You can turn it into matrix form by calling the corr method and save it as a variable:

```
tipsdata_corr = tips_data.corr()
```

This produces a dataset like the one below.

	total_bill	tip	size
total_bill	1.000000	0.675734	0.598315
tip	0.675734	1.000000	0.489299
size	0.598315	0.489299	1.000000

Now the column and the index name match up, i.e., total_bill

Now, to call a heatmap, you just call:

```
sns.heatmap(tipsdata_corr)
```

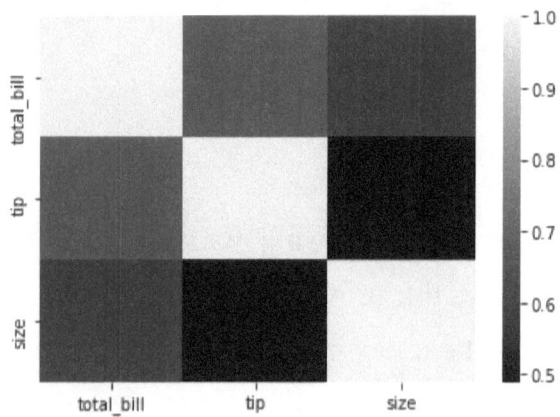

A heatmap colors the data points on a color gradient filter to produce the above representation. Heatmaps accepts other arguments such as `annot=Boolean,` this annotates the associated values with the plots as shown below.

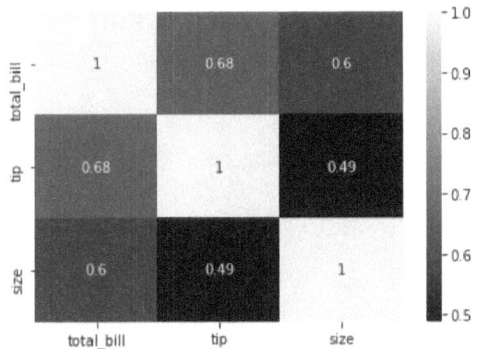

To convert the flights data into matrix form, you can use the pivot_table method to allocate every item in the dataset. The code is as follows

```
flight_pivot = flights_data.pivot_table(index='month', columns='year', values='passengers')
flight_pivot
```

year	1949	1950	1951	1952	1953	1954	1955	1956	1957	1958	1959	1960
month												
January	112	115	145	171	196	204	242	284	315	340	360	417
February	118	126	150	180	196	188	233	277	301	318	342	391
March	132	141	178	193	236	235	267	317	356	362	406	419
April	129	135	163	181	235	227	269	313	348	348	396	461
May	121	125	172	183	229	234	270	318	355	363	420	472
June	135	149	178	218	243	264	315	374	422	435	472	535
July	148	170	199	230	264	302	364	413	465	491	548	622
August	148	170	199	242	272	293	347	405	467	505	559	606
September	136	158	184	209	237	259	312	355	404	404	463	508
October	119	133	162	191	211	229	274	306	347	359	407	461
November	104	114	146	172	180	203	237	271	305	310	362	390
December	118	140	166	194	201	229	278	306	336	337	405	432

To visualize the data above using heatmap, just call heatmap() function on the flight_pivot data. This produces a heatmap as shown below. From this illustration, you can be able to tell which year had more flights and which month of the year.

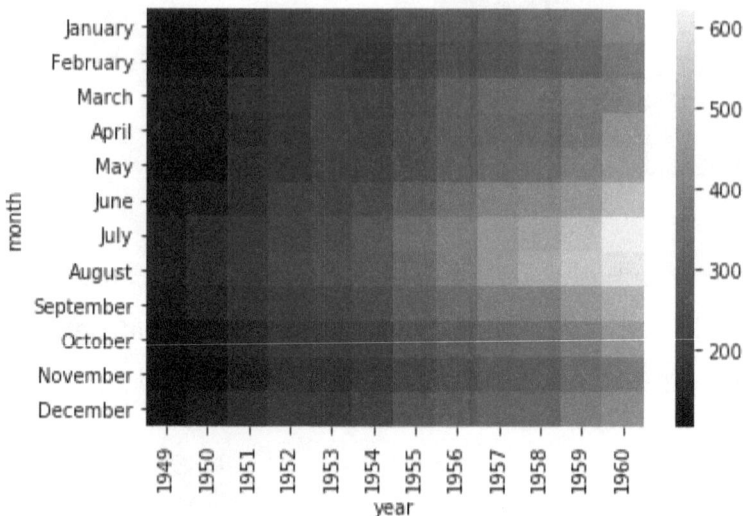

2: Cluster maps

Seaborn cluster maps use hierarchical clustering to produce a clustered version of a heatmap. Similar to any other type of matrix plot, your data should be in matrix form before calling `clustermap()` function.

An illustration of a cluster map of the flight data appears below:

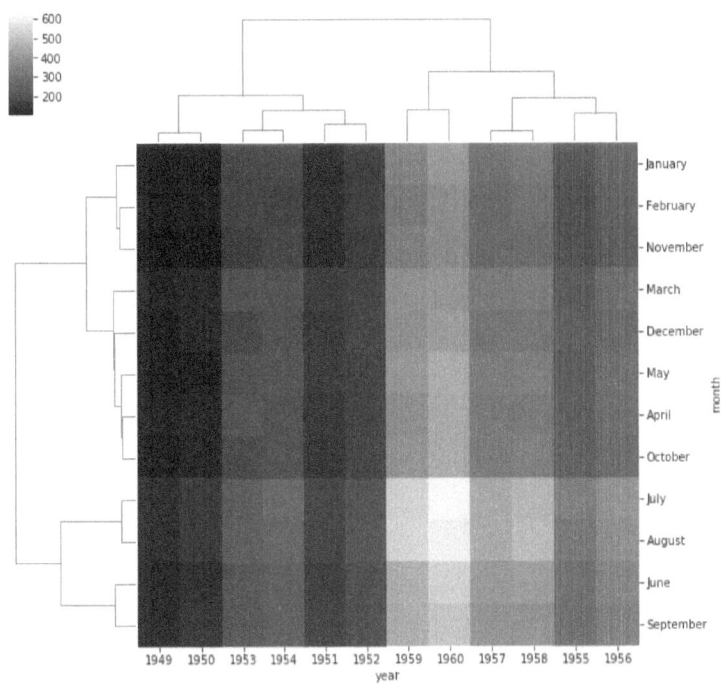

The above cluster-like bars try to cluster columns together based off their similarity. This makes data interpretation a little easier. You can conclude that year 1951 and 1952 are similar to each other.

3: Seaborn Grids

Let us start by importing seaborn. This time, we are going to use the diamonds dataset provided by seaborn.

```
import seaborn as sns

%matplotlib inline
```

```
diamonds = sns.read_dataset('diamonds')
```

```
diamonds.head()
```

You can use the pairplot feature to plot the above data automatically. Here, we are going to look at seaborn grid mechanism to customize the plots. We can do this by first calling the `PairGrid()` function.

```
sns.PairGrid(diamonds)
```

This provides you with a dozen of empty grids with no data. Now you have more control over the plotting system rather than using the pairplot, which does things automatically. This allows you to specify the type of plot you want on the diagonal, upper diagonal and lower half.

Regression plots

Seaborn supports different types of regression plots. Regression is a scientific algorithm that allows data scientists to predict continuous data. Regressions such as linear regression are applicable only in machine learning. Here, we are only going to cover the LM plot function that allows you to display linear models with Seaborn.

As usual, import Seaborn and load the tips dataset. To make a linear model plot off the tips data, call the:

```
sns.lmplot(x,y,data)
```

```
import seaborn as sns
%matplotlib inline
tips_data = sns.load_dataset('tips')
tips_data.head()
```

The code below shows a scatter plot with a linear fit inside.

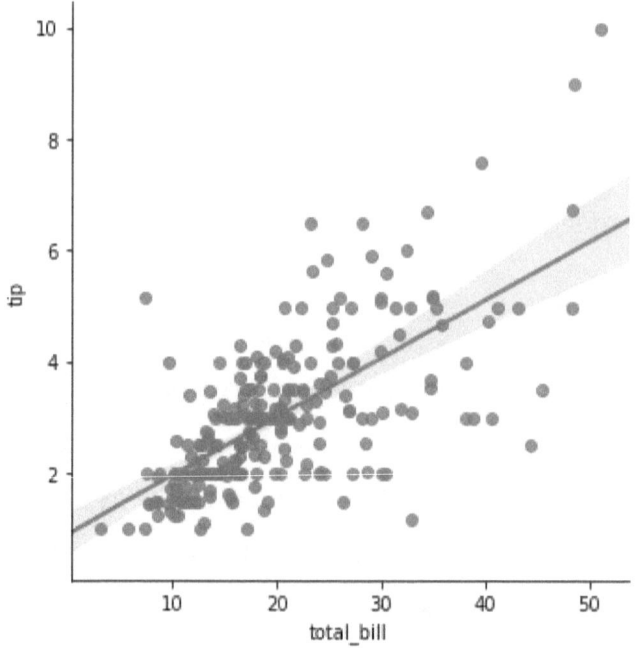

```
sns.lmplot(x='total_bill', y='tip', data=tips_data)
```

The linear models function supports some of Matplotlib parameters to affect the representation of the data.

Seaborn Styling and Colors

We have previously seen how to change the style and appearance of plots using various parameters. Now we are going to look at detailed styling features supported by Seaborn.

Let us start by importing Seaborn and the tips dataset.

First, try to create a scatterplot or any plot you would like. Let us go with bar plots:

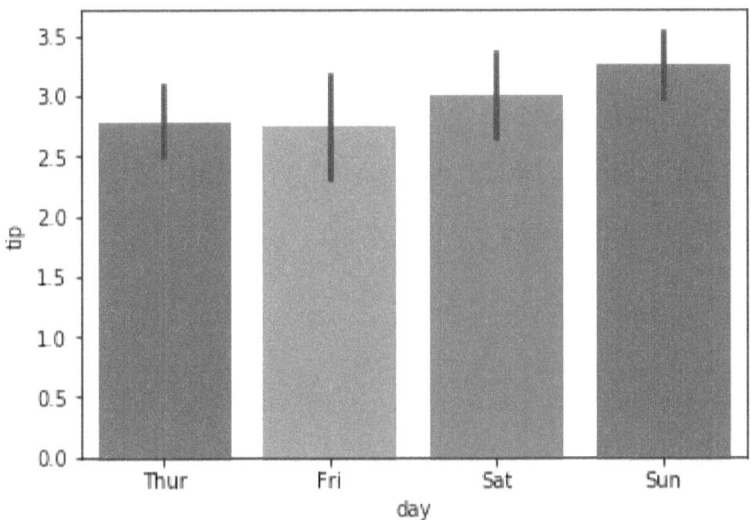

Seaborn has a style function used to control how the plots display:

```
sns.set_style(style_as_string)
```

The Seaborn style figures include:

❖ white

❖ dark

❖ darkgrid

❖ whitegrid

❖ ticks

Go ahead and try the styles to see which you prefer. Another Seaborn styling is spines. Spines are the sidebars displayed on a Seaborn plot. To remove them, use the `sns.despine()` function. This function allows you to remove all four spines by passing them as Boolean arguments. For example,

```
sns.despine(right=True,          left=True,
bottom=True, top=True)
```

By default, right and top parameters are usually set to true. This sets a figure like the one below.

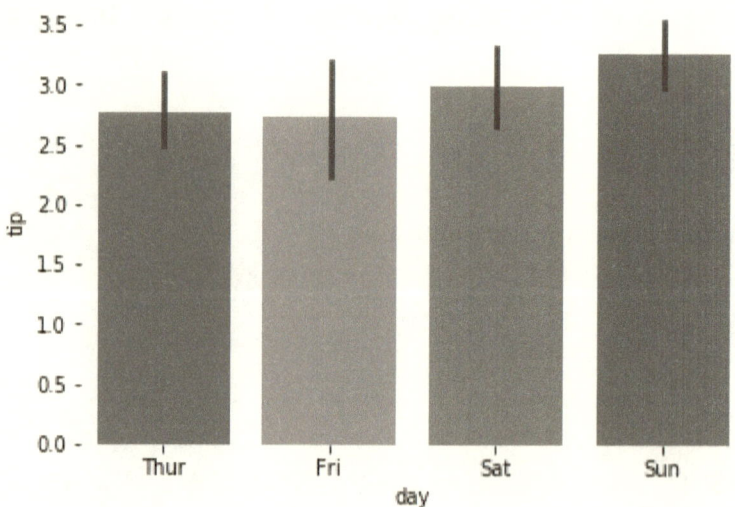

Since all Seaborn plots are just callbacks to the Matplotlib library, you can use the matplotlib `plt.figure(figsize=(width,height))` feature to set the aspect ratio of a seaborn plot.

Now that we have discussed how to analyze and visualize data using python scientific libraries, we can use the knowledge to perform data science operations using python.

Conclusion

This guidebook has equipped you with the basic knowledge you need to have to start using Python for data science. Like most programming aspects, mastery of the various elements we have discussed in this guidebook will only come from consistent practice. Practice what you have learned here every chance you get and without a doubt, you will be well on your way to being a great data scientist.

I'd like your feedback. If you are happy with this book, please leave a review on Amazon.

Please leave a review for this book on Amazon by visiting the page below:

https://amzn.to/2VMR5qr